HAMAS

Hamas
A Beginner's Guide
Second edition

Khaled Hroub

PLUTO PRESS

First published 2006. Second edition published 2010 by Pluto Press
345 Archway Road, London N6 5AA and
175 Fifth Avenue, New York, NY 10010

www.plutobooks.com

British Library Cataloguing in Publication Data
A catalogue record for this book is available from the British Library

ISBN   978 0 7453 2973 4   Hardback
ISBN   978 0 7453 2972 7   Paperback
ISBN   978 1 8496 4553 9   PDF eBook
ISBN   978 1 7837 1466 7   EPUB eBook
ISBN   978 1 7837 1467 4   Kindle eBook

Library of Congress Cataloging in Publication Data applied for

This book is printed on paper suitable for recycling and made from fully managed
and sustained forest sources. Logging, pulping and manufacturing processes are
expected to conform to the environmental standards of the country of origin.

10 9 8 7 6 5 4 3 2 1

Designed and produced for Pluto Press by
Curran Publishing Services, Norwich

Contents

[v]

Preface

Hamas used to make shocking news the world over by its suicide attacks at the hearts of Israeli cities – unreserved retaliation to the continuous Israeli attacks against Palestinian cities and people. With no less of an impact, Hamas shocked the world in an unexpected way on 25 January 2006 by winning a landslide victory in the elections of the Palestinian Legislative Council (PLC). The PLC, although a quasi-parliament with limited sovereign powers, represents the embodiment of Palestinian political legitimacy in the West Bank and Gaza Strip. By virtue of its victory Hamas formed a government and became the leading force in the national Palestinian struggle for the first time since it was founded in late 1987.

The result of the elections stunned the world. How could it be that a 'terrorist organization' as it is has always been labelled in the West, with a spooky secretive image, as it has been always portrayed in Western media, had emerged as a victorious popular political power? Hamas's main rival had been the secular Fatah movement, which had led the Palestinians for almost half a century almost without interruption. Israel, the United States, Europe, the Arab regimes, the UN and many other regional and international players wanted Fatah to win. Against all odds and enemies Hamas triumphed! The entire world bemoaned, 'What went wrong?'

In fact there was no 'right' against which 'wrong' could be measured in the context of the Palestinian elections. What went wrong, indeed, was the persistent and prevailing misconception of Hamas and the belittling of its power and leverage. Hamas in the eyes of many Westerners, official and lay alike, has always been reduced to a mere 'terrorist group' whose only function is and has been to aimlessly kill Israelis. On the ground in their own country, Hamas has been seen by many Palestinians as a deeply entrenched socio-political and popular force. In Palestinian eyes Hamas had been managing to chart parallel and harmonious paths of both military confrontation against the Israeli occupation, and grassroots social work, religious and ideological mobilisation and PR networking with other states and movements.

This book sets forth to tell the story of the 'real Hamas', not the misperceived and distorted one. By 'real Hamas' I mean the reality of Hamas as it has been on the ground in all its aspects – debunking any reductionist approach. Yet there is no intention here to provide an apologetic treatise about Hamas. It is up to the reader to shape her or his own opinion on this Palestinian movement. The purpose of this book, though, is to provide the basic information and necessary clarifying analysis.

The chapters of the book take the format of questions and answers, which may not seem very familiar. But it is in the interest of simplifying what could be seen by many as a complicated issue. Presenting the 'most frequently asked questions' about Hamas (within the Arab/Israeli conflict) and tackling them separately allows for a more straightforward and accessible read. The chapters are structured in both chronological and thematic fashion starting with the origins of Hamas and ending with the 'new Hamas' (Hamas after the elections), with all other aspects and issues relating to Hamas in between.

Over the past 16 years I have been following the developments of and within Hamas. I have written extensively on its social, political, military and religious aspects. I have published books, chapters in books, journal articles and many other writings trying to understand Hamas and convey my understanding to readers. I have interviewed Hamas's leaders and met many of its policy-makers. Based on my close knowledge and first hand contact with Hamas people, I have taken the liberty to free the text in this book from footnotes and tiring references. In my other works such referencing and documentation is widely available, if sought.

My own perception of Hamas goes beyond the mere question of being with or against the movement. As a secular person myself, my aspiration is for Palestine, and all other Arab countries for that matter, to be governed by human-made laws. However, I see Hamas as a natural outcome of un-natural, brutal occupational conditions. The radicalism of Hamas should be seen as a completely predictable result of the ongoing Israeli colonial project in Palestine. Palestinians support whichever movement holds the banner of resistance against that occupation and promises to defend the Palestinian rights of freedom and self-determination. At this juncture of history, they see in Hamas the defender of those rights.

Words of gratitude are indeed due at the outset to family, friends and colleagues whose efforts and help make the publication of this book possible. I thank Roger van Zwanenberg of Pluto Books for his encouragement and friendly persistence to have me write this book. I also thank the staff at Pluto Books who put great effort in the production process of the book, Melanie Patrick, Helen Griffiths, Alec Gregory and Susan Curran from Curran Publishing. My sincere thanks go to my Cambridge friend and editor Pam Manix who stood by me chapter by chapter, glued to her computer during all those late nights of writing the book. I also thank Abed al-Juebeh, my dear friend and colleague at al-Jazeera, for his support and help. The ongoing insightful discussions with him, along with his critical and sometimes cynical mind were sources of inspiration for me. The final thanks and love go to my precious small family: Kholoud my wife and friend and my children Laith and Mayce, who as ever endured the little time I've given to them during the writing of this book, yet surrounded me with love, warmth and affection.

Introduction

In January 2006 Hamas stunned the world by winning the democratic elections for the Palestinian Legislative Council of the limited Palestinian Authority in the West Bank and the Gaza Strip. Bringing Hamas into the unprecedented glare of the limelight, this victory shocked many Palestinians, Israel, the United States, Europe and Arab countries. It also left the defeated Palestinian Fatah movement, Hamas's main rival which had led the Palestinian national movement for more than 40 years, completely shattered.

Despite the shock and surprise, Hamas's victory in those elections was in fact almost unavoidable. The cumulative failure over the past years to end a continuing brutal Israeli occupation of Palestinian land and people had only deepened the frustration and radicalism within the Palestinian people. Palestinian frustration and suffering has never ended since the creation of Israel by war in 1948. With British collusion and American support and against the will and interest of the native population, the piece of land that had been known for many hundreds of years as Palestine became Israel. In this war to create Israel the Palestinians lost more than 78 per cent of the land of Palestine, including the western part of their capital Jerusalem. What remained to the Palestinians were two separate pieces of land known as the West Bank (of the Jordan River) adjacent to the country of Jordan, which included a fragment of their old capital city, East Jerusalem, and the Gaza Strip on the Mediterranean bordering the Egyptian Sinai peninsula. As a

result of the 1948 war, hundreds of thousands of Palestinians
were driven out from their cities and villages to neighbouring
countries by Zionist forces. These 'refugees' have become the
most intractable problem of the conflict, growing in numbers
with their descendants to more than 6 million by the year 2006.

In 1967 Israel launched another successful war, this time
not just against the Palestinians but also against all the bordering Arab countries as well. Palestinian losses were nearly
complete. With this war Israel occupied the West Bank and the
eastern part of Jerusalem, which had been under Jordanian rule,
and the Gaza Strip, which had been administered by Egypt
since the 1948 war. Israel also invaded Syria's Golan Heights in
the north, and Egypt's Sinai desert in the South, and staunchly
occupied them all in the name of Israeli security. Yet for the
Palestinians the losses were multiple. The Israeli army forced
another mass transfer of Palestinians refugees, this time from
the West Bank cities and villages to neighbouring countries.
Many of the refugees who had been uprooted to the West Bank
during the 1948 war were moved on yet again, and with even
more new refugees because of the 1967 war. The problem of
Palestinian refugees had worsened.

Weakened Arab countries, along with the nascent Palestinian national liberation movement, failed in their military efforts
to regain the land they had lost to Israel in 1967. Two years
prior to that war, Yasser Arafat and other Palestinian activists in
the West Bank and Gaza Strip and neighbouring Arab countries
established Fatah, the Palestinian national liberation movement.
Fatah declared a no-ideology affiliation and a secular outlook.
Around the same time, and with other smaller leftist factions,
the Palestine Liberation Organization (PLO) was established as
a national umbrella front for the Palestinian struggle, with the
clear leadership of Fatah. The goal of the PLO was to 'liberate
Palestine': that was to say, the land that had been occupied in
the war of 1948 and which had become known as Israel. Yet
after the devastating loss of the West Bank and Gaza Strip in

1967, the goal of the PLO had to be reduced. Instead of 'liberating Palestine' it focused on the liberation of only the two more recently lost parts of the land, the West Bank and the Gaza Strip. This goal was seen at this time merely as an intermediate phase which would not affect the long-term goal of liberating the entire land of Palestine.

From the mid-1960s to almost the mid-1980s the PLO-led Palestinian national movement embraced armed struggle as the principal strategy to 'liberate Palestine'. Arab weakness coupled with continuous international and Western support of Israel made the Palestinians' mission of liberating their land almost impossible. Achieving no success over decades of struggle, the PLO made two historic concessions by the end of the 1980s. It relinquished its long-term goal – the 'liberation of Palestine' – by recognizing Israel and its right to exist. It also dropped the armed struggle as a strategy, for the sake of a negotiated settlement that hoped to regain the West Bank and the Gaza Strip and establish an independent Palestinian state.

In 1991 the United States convened the Madrid Peace Conference in the aftermath of the first Gulf War and the expulsion of Saddam Hussein's troops from Kuwait. With Arabs everywhere fragmented because of the Iraqi invasion of Kuwait, the ensuing war, and a weakened Palestinian position because the PLO had sided (verbally and politically) with Iraq against the American-led coalition troops, the PLO's negotiating position in Madrid was fragile. Not unexpectedly, the Conference failed to produce a Palestinian/Israeli peace treaty, but succeeded in confirming the historic shift on the side of the PLO towards negotiation instead of armed struggle as its preferred strategy to end the conflict.

In 1993 an initial agreement was reached between the PLO and Israel, the Oslo Agreement, after months of secret talks in Norway. Endorsed in Washington by the Clinton Administration, the agreement was in theory divided into two phases: a five-year interim phase (essentially meant to explore and test

the competence of the Palestinians to peacefully rule themselves and control 'illegal' armed resistance factions) starting in
1994, which if it proved successful would be followed by a
second phase of negotiations on a 'final settlement'. The Palestinians were almost evenly divided in response to the Oslo
Accords. Those who supported Oslo argued that it was the best
deal that the Palestinians could hope to achieve given the
unfavourable conditions they faced and the tilted balance of
power that remained unassailably propitious to Israel. Those
who opposed it argued that it simply constituted surrender to
Israel, by recognizing the Israeli state and officially dropping
the armed struggle without any concrete gains. In the five-year
interim period there was to be no addressing any of the major
Palestinian issues such the right of refugees to return, the status
of Jerusalem, the control over Palestinian borders, and the
dismantling of the Israeli settlements build intensively in the
occupied West Bank and the Gaza Strip. According to the
Accords, these issues were all to be relegated to the final talks,
which as it turned out, would never take place anyway.

Hamas has consistently opposed the Oslo Agreement,
believing that it was designed to serve Israeli interests and
compromised basic Palestinian rights. After more than ten years
of Oslo, the Palestinians had become completely frustrated and
their initial shaky trust in the sincerity of peace talks with Israel
had evaporated. During the interim period of years that would
supposedly pave the way for permanent peace, Israel did every-
thing possible to worsen the life of Palestinians and enhance its
colonial occupation of the West Bank and Gaza Strip. During
that period of time, for example, the size and number of Israeli
colonial settlements in the West Bank – a major obstacle facing
any final peace agreement – doubled. With the failure of Oslo,
a second *intifada* erupted in 2000 against Israel, giving more
power and influence to Hamas and its 'resistance project'.

In March 2005 Hamas made three successive historic decisions, each of which represents a milestone in the movement's

political life. The movement decided to run for the Palestinian Legislative Council elections in the West Bank and Gaza Strip. It decided that along with other Palestinian factions it would put on hold all military activities, for an unspecified amount of time and on its own terms. And it considered joining the PLO.

Hamas seemed to have decided to move firmly towards the top of the Palestinian leadership. The most important of these three milestones was Hamas's decision to participate in the legislative elections in January 2006. This decision was completely in the opposite direction to its previous refusal to take part in 1996 elections because Hamas perceived them as an outcome of the Oslo Accords. By way of justification of the new move it put forward the new conditions since the September 2000 *intifada*. Hamas was also becoming confident of its own strength, after having won almost two-thirds of the seats in the January 2005 partial municipal elections.

Hamas's decision to take part in the elections had a profound impact on the nature of the movement, on the Palestinian political scene and on the peace process at large. At the level of its internal make-up, it would help politicize the movement – at the expense of its well-known militarism.

HAMAS

Founded in the late 1980s, Hamas emerged as a doubly driven religious-nationalist liberation movement which peacefully preaches the Islamic religious call while harmoniously embracing the strategy of armed struggle against an occupying Israel. Its critics thought it seemed as if Hamas started where the PLO had left off. Its supporters felt that Hamas came at just the right time to salvage the Palestinian national struggle from complete capitulation to Israel. On the ground, Hamas hacked its own path in almost the opposite direction to the peaceful route then being taken by the PLO and other Arab countries that had concluded peace treaties with Israel, namely Egypt and Jordan. It refused to come under the PLO as the wider umbrella of the Palestinian nationalist struggle, and adopted the 'old' call for the 'liberation of Palestine' as it had been originally enshrined by the PLO founders back in the mid-1960s. Hamas rejected the idea of concluding peace treaties with Israel that were conditional on full Palestinian recognition of the right of Israel to exist.

With the lack of any serious breakthrough toward achieving even a minimum level of Palestinian rights, Hamas has sustained a continuous rise since its inception. After years of persistent struggle it has become a key player both within the parameters of the Arab and Palestinian-Israeli conflict and in the arena of political Islam in the region. At the Palestinian level, it has shown a continuing popular appeal. By using myriad and interconnected strategies spanning military attacks, educational, social and charitable work in addition to religious propagation, it has succeeded in popularizing itself across the Palestinian constituencies inside and outside Palestine. With the gradual erosion of both the legitimacy and popularity of the PLO, Hamas's power has manifested itself in landslide victories in municipal elections, student union elections, syndicational and other elections held in the West Bank and the Gaza Strip.

In the area of political Islam and its various approaches to politics, Hamas has offered a unique contemporary case of an Islamist movement that is engaged in a liberation struggle against a foreign occupation. Islamist movements have been driven by a host of various causes, the vast majority of which were focused on the corrupt regimes of their own countries. Another stream of movements, the 'globalized Jihadists', have expanded their 'holy campaigns' across geopolitical lines, furthering pan-Islamic notions that reject ideas of individual Muslim nation-states. Contrary to both of these, Hamas has somehow remained nation-state based, limiting its struggle to one for and within Palestine, and fighting not a local regime but a foreign occupier. This differentiation is important as it exposes the shallowness of the widespread (mostly Western) trivializing conflation of all Islamist movements into one single 'terrorist' category.

Hamas has undergone various developments and experiences, and there are clear maturational differences between its early years and its later phases. Over the years of the struggle, at historic junctures and decisive and sensitive turning points, Hamas has offered not only a fascinating case for study but more importantly a case of an emerging key player capable of affecting the course and the outcome of the Palestinian–Israeli conflict.

Vacillating between its strong religious foundations and political nationalist agendas, Hamas strives to keep a balance between its ultimate vision and immediate pressing realties. Although it will remain an open question to what extent the 'religious' and the 'political' constitute the make-up of Hamas, it is significant to witness the interplay between these two drives within the movement. Although the movement suppresses any implicit or explicit tension between the two, it is perhaps only a question of time and space, and the nature of certain events, before one of them succeeds in overriding the other. At the highly politicized junctures of Hamas's life, it has been clearly evident that the 'political' vigorously occupies the driver's seat.

Militarily, Hamas adopted the controversial tactic of 'suicide bombing', to which its name has become attached in the West and the rest of the world. The first use of this tactic was in 1994, in retaliation for a massacre of Palestinians praying in a mosque in the Palestinian city of Hebron. A fanatical Jewish settler opened machine gun fire upon the worshippers, killing 29 and injuring many more. Hamas vowed to revenge these killings, and so it did. Since then all and each of Hamas's vicious attacks against Israeli civilians have been directly linked to specific Israeli atrocities against Palestinian civilians.

Although no more brutal than what the Israelis have been doing to Palestinians for decades, the suicide attacks have damaged the reputation of both Hamas and the Palestinians worldwide. Hamas's justification for conducting these kinds of operation has many grounds. First, it says that these operations are the exception to the rule and only driven by the need to retaliate. It is an 'eye for an eye' policy in response to the continual killing of Palestinian civilians by the Israeli army. Second, Hamas says that it keeps extending an offer to Israel by which civilians on both sides would be spared from being targeted, but Israel has never accepted this offer. Third, Hamas leaders say that Israeli society as a whole should pay the price of the occupation of the West Bank and Gaza Strip, just as much as Palestinian society is paying the price for that occupation: fear and suffering should be felt on both sides.

At the socio-cultural level, Hamas has had mixed fortunes. Its grassroots social work in helping the poor and supporting hundreds of thousands of Palestinians has been admired and praised. This sustained work, which has been marked by competence and dedicated sincerity, has bestowed on the movement a high level of popularity. At election times this has paid off considerably. Combined with its military and confrontational action against Israel, Hamas has been functioning on several fronts at the same time, and this has not failed to impress the Palestinians.

However, many secular Palestinians have feared that Hamas has been indirectly, if incrementally, transforming the cultural and social fabric of Palestinian society. Hamas has seemingly exploited its socio-political capital and popularity to advance its cultural and religious agenda. Although there have been only a few occasions when Hamas members have attempted to impose certain religious morals on society, and these cannot really be described as a phenomenon, they have been enough to create anxiety among more secular Palestinians. Many Palestinians support the nationalist/liberationalist and social work of Hamas, but not its religious ideal. Hamas purposefully overlooks this fact, and instead considers any vote for its political agenda as a vote for its religious one too.

HAMAS IN POWER

The reasons behind the Hamas victory in the 2006 Palestinian Legislative Council (PLC) elections, and the significance of this victory, merit a closer look. Hamas triumphed for a host of reasons. In the first place the movement has indeed reaped the benefits of long years of devoted work and popularity among the Palestinians. At least half the voters supported Hamas for its programme and its declared objectives; also for its warmth and the helping hands that it has kept close to the poor and needy. The other half of Hamas's voters were driven by other forces. The failure of the peace process, combined with the ever-increasing brutality of the Israeli occupation, left the Palestinians with no faith in the option of negotiating a peaceful settlement with Israel. The gap in the debate on 'peace talks versus resistance' was closing as the date of the election approached, with the notion of 'peace talks' losing ground, yet without clear and definite support for Hamas's 'resistance' concept either. The latter was vague, and many Palestinians were wary about its meaning and mechanisms. But the frustration of the peace talks had by then taken its toll, and contributed largely to the defeat of the Fatah movement, the upholder and main force of the Oslo Agreements and what had resulted from them.

Another major factor that helped Hamas in winning those elections was the failure of the Fatah-led Palestinian Authority in almost in all aspects. It failed not only externally, on the front of the peace talks with Israel, but also internally, with its management of day-to-day services to the Palestinian people. Mismanagement, corruption and theft were the 'attributes' that came to mark Fatah's top leaders, ministers and high-ranking staff. As unemployment and poverty reached unprecedented levels, the extravagant lifestyle of senior Palestinian officials infuriated the public. The elections gave the people the chance to punish those officials. The chickens were coming home to roost, and Hamas was to be the beneficiary.

Thus, it can hardly be said that the Palestinian people voted for Hamas primarily on religious grounds. There was certainly no overnight popular conversion to Hamas's religious fervour or even its political ideology. Christians and secular people voted for Hamas side by side with Hamas members and exponents in all constituencies. Hamas's support of Christian candidates won them seats in the parliament. A Christian was appointed to the Hamas cabinet as the minister of tourism. The vast spectrum of Hamas's voters in these elections supported the suggestion that the people were voting for new blood, and for a nationalist liberation movement that promised change and reform on all fronts, more than for Hamas the religious group.

The Hamas election victory itself represents something significant not only for Palestinians but also for other Arabs, Muslims and beyond. At the Palestinian level it is a historic turning point, where a major shift has taken place in the leadership of the national liberation movement. For the first time in more than half a century Palestinian Islamists have moved into the driver's seat of the Palestinian national movement. It seems that almost overnight the Islamists have replaced the long-lived secular leadership that controlled the destiny of the Palestinians and their national decision making for decades. This fundamental change, furthermore, was realized through peaceful means and without violence, giving Palestinians as a whole – including Hamas – a great sense of pride. Not only are the Palestinians theoretically competent and ready to practise democratic rule, they have done so by embracing democracy on the ground and accepting its outcome. Moreover, the campaigns for the elections with their contrasting platforms gave the Palestinians the chance to revisit their strategy over the conflict with

Israel, as it had previously been designed and pursued by the Fatah movement.

For Hamas itself, this victory is the greatest challenge that the movement has faced since its emergence. Almost abruptly, all Hamas's ideals and slogans have been brought down to earth to face the harsh realities on the ground. It could be safely said that the post-election Hamas will be considerably different from the organization we used to know before the elections. At the Arab and Muslim level, Hamas's victory is almost unique: political Islam has reached power in a democratic process and will not be deprived of its victory. Islamist movements throughout the region were jubilant at Hamas's triumph and considered it to be their own victory. Existing Arab and Muslim regimes, on the other hand, have watched the rise of Hamas to power with obvious anxiety and suspicion, and fear that it will encourage their local Islamists to vigorously pursue power. Secular constituencies and individuals in the Arab countries remain divided. They support the nationalist liberation side of Hamas, but they continue to be agitated by its religious and social substance.

At the international level, a Palestinian government led by Hamas has been a most unwelcome phenomenon among the fruits of democracy. The West in particular is now caught in the dilemma of either accepting this disquieting result, to show the Arab and Muslim world that its call for democracy in the region is sincere, or joining Israeli efforts to bring down Hamas's government and risk losing credibility. The West decided early on to join the blockade on the new Hamas government, as part of a concerted effort by Israel, the United States, the European Union, some Arab states and the Fatah movement to oust it.

Strategically, many Palestinians have looked at Hamas's victory as benefiting the ultimate ends of the Palestinian national- ist movement in both the short and long term. Hamas's presence at the heart of the Palestinian decision-making mechanism furnishes further, and much needed, legitimacy to the Palestinian

Authority. It also brings more integrity and trust to the entire make-up of Palestinian politics. Hamas had never previously participated in the Palestinian Authority constructed by the Oslo Accords, on the basis that both the Accords and the Authority had capitulated to Israel and made unacceptable concessions. Capitalizing on a 'free-ride' type of discourse, Hamas has not only succeeded in amassing astonishing popularity: it also challenged the leading position of Fatah, the backbone of the PLO and the strongest party in mainstream Palestinian society. The inclusion of Hamas in the political process will now deprive Fatah of the erstwhile free-ride politics it came to abuse, and ensure it is held responsible for more 'real' politics along with other Palestinian parties.

More importantly, and at the level of the conflict with Israel, there cannot be a sustainable and final peace deal without a real Palestinian consensus, to which Hamas's contribution is central. Hamas's political position is pragmatic and hovers around accepting the concept of a two-state solution. If a decent final agreement can be reached, recognizing Palestinian rights according to Madrid Conference references and UN resolutions, Hamas will be unable to object. A moderate, co-opted and participating Hamas, even if it hardens the PA position, is far better than a radicalized and militarized Hamas.

Introduction to the Second Edition

WESTERN ENGAGEMENT WITH HAMAS?

Two years after the blockade of the Gaza Strip, Mahmoud Zahhar, a prominent Hamas leader in Gaza, wrote in the *Washington Post* (on 17 April 2008) the following: 'Sixty-five years ago, the courageous Jews of the Warsaw ghetto rose in defense of their people. We Gazans, living in the World's largest open-air prison, can do no less.' It is not only this statement but also the developments on the ground over the four years since Hamas won the elections in 2006 which have confirmed one thing: the refusal to accept that is necessary to engage with Hamas has been devastating by all measures political and human, and almost exclusively for the Palestinians.

Here is an irony followed by an ironic question: the majority of Israelis support direct talks with Hamas, but the 'international community' does not! According to a *Ha'aretz*-Dialogue poll conducted in March 2008, 64 per cent of Israelis say that their leaders 'must hold direct talks with the Hamas government in Gaza toward a cease-fire and the release of captive soldier Gilad Shalit [captured by Hamas in June 2006]'. Another poll in November 2009 showed that 57 per cent of Israelis supported a plan proposed by Shaul Mofaz, the second-ranking leader of the Israeli Kadima party, which includes talking to Hamas. The ironic question that follows has a British flavour, alas, and ponders the experience and lessons of the direct and indirect talks with the IRA, as revealed in a book by Tony Blair's chief of staff, Jonathan Powell. The two main lessons concluded in Powell's *Great Hatred, Little Room: Making peace in Northern Ireland* (2008) were the need to 'talk to the enemies' and to 'create consensus on their front' which could lead to a consensual negotiated agreement. These two common-sense lessons are not hard to learn. Yet both have been discarded by the British and other Western governments, let alone Israel, in their dealing with Hamas. The consequences of their 'no-talking' policy have proved to be scandalous on the Western side and disastrous for the Palestinians.

Responding to Hamas's surprising victory in the January 2006 Palestinian elections, Europe joined an American-led effort to boycott Hamas and its subsequent government. The Western capitals, along with Tel Aviv, have thereafter imposed on Hamas a set of conditions that the movement had to meet if it wanted Hamas and its electoral victory to be acknowledged by the 'international community'. In fact it would not have been possible for the movement to completely fulfil those conditions unless it were to agree to dispose of the very cards that made its democratic election victory possible: in other words, to volun-tarily commit political suicide. In fact the movement went a long way toward risking doing just that, as 'Hamas in power' stretched itself and its positions half-way by agreeing to meet the three conditions of 'recognizing Israel', 'renouncing terror-ism' and 'adhering to previous agreements between Israel and the Palestinian Authority'. Repeatedly official Hamas state-ments have accepted the two-state solution principle, constitut-ing a de facto (if not spoken) recognition of Israel. Hamas announced a unilateral truce by which it stopped all its military activities until Israel resumed its incursions and attacks against the Gaza Strip; and it declared in a statement of the national unity government in March 2007 its 'respect' for previous agreements between Israel and the Palestine Liberation Organization (PLO). For Washington and Brussels those incremental moves by Hamas were not enough. Yet Hamas could stretch no further, otherwise it would have jeopardized its own unity and coherence. What the West refuses to see is that this also brings jeopardy to themselves, as a first disunited, and then fragmented Hamas would unleash a complete Iraqization of the Gaza Strip and a wholesale catastrophic situation.

Hamas's failure after its election victory to bring about political achievements which would have offset the rising anger within its own ranks, especially from the idle military, was exacerbated by the enormous pressures and crippling interdictions coming from external players. To make things worse, some influential Fatah leaders and groups in the Gaza Strip vowed to create further security chaos in an effort to bring Hamas's government down. All the conditions, internally and externally, were ripe, and they precipitated Hamas's pre-emptive, violent military take-over of Gaza in June 2007 – displacing the remaining Fatah leadership, and controlling all security forces – which has led to an unprecedented political and geographical split between Palestinians.

The greatest opportunity to appear during the span of the four years following Hamas's electoral victory was the short-lived national unity government of 2007. Brokered by the Saudis after the intensification of Fatah/Hamas clashes in the Strip, this government offered, for the first time in over 20 years, a chance for the creation of a viable Palestinian consensus. However, Western positions towards the unity government did not change despite the extra mile that Hamas had gone toward meeting the West. The stances of the United States and the European Union lacked not only insightfulness but also the required sense of pragmatism. This complete lack of support for the unity government by the West drove Hamas further to the edge, forcing them to seek more support from Iran and Syria. The national unity government represented the great missed chance to bring the movement back into the fold of internal Palestinian politics, where the focus would be driven by exclusive Palestinian interests. Had the Palestinians been encouraged by the United States and the European Union, if not pressured, to have a unified leadership – with Fatah and Hamas at the heart of it – the road forward to making peace would have been better paved. By way of comparison, creating a national consensus and broader platform of polity is precisely what the United States and the European Union have been trying to achieve in Iraq. But not so in Palestine.

Since the emergence of Hamas in 1987 the Palestinian polity has been divided into a 'peace camp' and a 'resistance camp'. These function in complete disharmony, and the resultant effort of these two camps has been more harmful to the Palestinians than to Israel. With the signing of the Oslo Agreements in 1993/4 the rift between the two approaches had become wider and deeper. The 'Northern Ireland' commonsense lesson of creating consensus on the 'other side' suggests that the inclusion of Hamas in the Palestinian political process would have been a vital condition for any potential peace and consensual agreement. Yet this lesson was ignored, in favour of the premise of leaving the Palestinian leadership, dependent upon Arafat's charisma and power at the top of it, with the business of selling (or imposing) any reached deal on the Palestinians. No 'promised' deal was ever reached, and now Arafat is not around and gone with him is any potential of him imposing a deal. Even if there ever was any validity in the logic of 'imposing' a consensus-lacking peace deal on the Palestinians, particularly one relying on an individual charismatic leadership, it now has no credibility whatsoever given the sheer weakness of the current Palestinian president Mamoud Abbas and the unyielding power of Hamas and its political/electoral legitimacy. This is why the format of any Israeli/Palestinian negotiations that excludes Hamas is rendered obsolete. Even if a semi-miracle happened and an agreement was concluded by

Israel and the Palestinian president, who would implement it, and how, in the Gaza Strip without Hamas's approval?

The hard-learned Northern Ireland lessons of dealing with the enemy are not showing up in Western foreign policy, in Palestine at least. At one point during the conclusion of the Palestinian national unity government, according to a Hamas source, there were some signals coming from London that Ismail Haniyeh, Hamas's prime minister, would have been invited to London along with the Palestinian president after the official declaration of government. Such a step, if it was really on the horizon, would have helped change the violent course of events that unfolded in the following weeks. It could have given a measure of international legitimacy to Hamas's leadership which it could have sold to its constituencies, and equally driven back those reckless Fatah leaders in the Gaza Strip who thought that Hamas's days in government were numbered. The same Hamas source went on to say that London eventually backtracked and refrained from inviting any Hamas minister, as did some other European Union countries. In Europe it is always said that the Palestinian president and some Arab governments, primarily Egypt and Jordan, pressured the Europeans to shut Hamas out even after the national unity government was formed. This pressure is not a surprise, though it is ironic that such weak governments, internally and regionally, could have the power to 'pressure' the European Union. Nevertheless, the real surprise is that the Western capitals yielded to the pressure.

Talking to Hamas also falls within a wider scheme of thinking about the rising power of Islamists in the Middle East. The key word here is engagement. And the argument is that Western governments should talk and engage with Hamas and other Islamist movements, especially when they are democratically elected and show readiness and eagerness for dialogue. The Turkish model has some wisdom to offer. The 'European agenda' of the government of the Turkish Justice and Development Party

(AKP), with its Islamist background and constituency, has affected the total orientation and moderation of the party. Engagement, of course, may not change policies full scale and in short periods of time; that should be clearly acknowledged. But it certainly moderates people and blunts the edges of their radicalism.

Europe and in particular Britain have had a historically peculiar role to play in the Middle East, in the past and present. When it comes to Palestine, most Palestinians hold Britain responsible for originating their long-lived misery. It is the 'Balfour Declaration' of 1917, by which the Jews were promised a homeland in Palestine by the British colonial power, that digs deep into the Palestinian psyche and is considered by many of them to be the 'mother of all these sins'. Britain shoulders a fair share of the historical responsibility for what happened to the Palestinians, and it should equally carry an equivalent share of the burden for relieving their current situation. Alas, what frustrates many Palestinians, and not only Hamas, is to see Britain and Europe merely reproducing American positions which are biased against their cause.

Despite all appearances, Hamas has not strayed too far from politics. It might be on the edge but there is still a good chance of bringing Hamas back into the fold before it is too late. Weakening Hamas provides space for more radical splinter groups attempting to emulate al-Qaeda tactics. Yet even the strategy of finishing off Hamas by excessive military means, and even the forms of war crimes as we have seen in the December 2008/January 2009 Israeli war, proved failures. The facts on the ground say that Hamas is there to stay, for it is not a marginal alienated group on the fringes of the Palestinian society. It is a mainstream movement which won free and fair elections. The Gaza war aftermath has if anything proved the Hamas steadfastness that Zahhar's statement to the *Washington Post* asserted.

1 Hamas's history

ISLAMISM AND THE PALESTINIAN STRUGGLE

How are Islam and Palestine interrelated?

Over the centuries, Islam and Palestine have been intimately linked in the imagery and history of Muslims. Palestine has been bestowed with Islamic holiness, as well as religious significance for Christian and Jewish people, for a host of reasons and historic events. Jerusalem, and in particular *al-Masjid al-Aqsa* (the furthest mosque), is the first place to which Muslims directed their prayers when the Prophet Muhammad started preaching Islam in Arabia in the early seventh century. *Bait al-Maqdes*, or Jerusalem, is the third holiest places in Islam after Mecca and Medina in Arabia. It is frequently referred to in the *Quran,* and is given numerous mentions in the sayings – *Hadith* – of the Prophets. Most of the stories about God's messengers as related in the Quran have specific geographical references to Palestine. One full chapter in the *Quran, sourat al-Isra,* is dedicated to the Prophet Muhammad's journey from Mecca to Jerusalem, and his ascension there to heaven to meet God. This is a chapter passionately embraced by Muslims the world over as one of the most astonishing divine stories. On the very rock where the Prophet set off on his journey to heaven, the Dome of the Rock was built, adjacent to the spot where the Jews say the Old Temple of Solomon was built.

The Christian and Jewish religious significance of Palestine is also recognized in Islam. Jesus Christ, who was born in Palestine, and Moses, who migrated to it, are considered by the *Quran* and Muslims to be two of the five most highly regarded prophets of God (the other three being Muhammad, Ibrahim and Ismail).

Added to its religious sacredness, Palestine has long occupied a geo-strategic position, linking the African and Asian parts of the Middle East, offering a long coast and rich passage on the Mediterranean between the Arabian peninsula, Egypt and Greater Syria. Because of its religious and strategic significance Palestine was destined to be the field of wars and invasions. Muslims conquered Palestine and brought it under their control in 638 AD. Since then Islam has been a central feature of the political, cultural and emotional foundation of this ancient tract of land.

The Western Crusaders from 1097 onward for two hundred years fought war after war to gain control over Palestine, and in particular Jerusalem, and bring it within Christendom. The Muslims, who at that point already had ruled Palestine for over 400 years, had long allowed people of other religions to live in peace in their lands. Muslims had long welcomed pilgrims of all religions, and had made accessible all of the historical shrines of religious significance to themselves and others: Christians, Jews, Persians, Orthodox Christians, Coptics and many others. Palestine was part of an ancient area, sacred to many people.

After 400 years of open exchange, and to the humiliation of Muslims, the Crusaders ruthlessly took Jerusalem, slaughtered its Muslim inhabitants and succeeded in ruling there for 70 years. When Saladin defeated the Crusaders in 1187 AD he entered the imagination and history of Islam as one of its most prominent heroes, whose successes signified the end of Muslim disgrace and defeat. The name of Saladin brings to Muslims and Palestinians memories of glory, and for many of them it emphasizes the inevitable will and capacity to rise from the ashes. Perceived as brutal foreign invasions launched by European Christians, the Crusades are still seen by many Arabs and Palestinians as the original blueprint for the Zionist invasion, which also had its roots in Europe.

What is the relationship between Islam and Palestine within the Arab–Israeli conflict?

In the consciousness of many Muslims, the identity of the ruler of Palestine indicates the strength or weakness of Islam and Muslims. If Palestine is ruled and controlled by foreigners and non-Muslims – from the Crusaders of the medieval ages to the Zionists of the twentieth century and the present – then Islam and Muslims perceive themselves to be weak and defeated.

After the final defeat of the Crusaders in 1291, Palestine remained under Muslim rule for over 700 additional years, until the break-up of the Muslim Ottoman Empire which had ruled Palestine, in the aftermath of World War I. The collapse of this declining Turkish empire, which had sided with the German allies in the Great War, was met with scant specific regret and loyalty by many in Palestine and the rest of the Arab world, because of the recent brutality of its reign. However the Ottoman foundation in Islam had kept Palestine firmly fixed within the Arab and Muslim world.

With the complete political collapse of the Empire in the wake of the armistice, Ottoman territories in the Middle East were carved up into temporary protectorates controlled by the European victors, until more permanent political configurations could be concluded. A temporary British mandate was set up over Palestine between 1922 and 1948. While the centuries-long roots of Islamic heritage and allegiance in Palestine were self-evident, strong currents of Zionism had long infiltrated British thinking. As early as 1917 Balfour had expressed his intention to support a Jewish national homeland in Palestine, and with the surge of Jewish refugees fleeing increasingly larger Nazi-controlled parts of Europe, Jewish immigration into British-administered Palestine escalated throughout the 1930s and 1940s.

Fighting what were clearly perceived to be colonial powers, Arab liberation movements across the former Ottoman territories united across their assorted versions of Islam and individual nationalism, and attempted to maximize the mobilization capacities of both tenets. In Palestine, Palestinians revolted against the British mandate during the 1920s and 1930s under just such a blended Islamic banner.

But the fate of Palestine would be irrevocably compounded by factors beyond the simple struggle between colonizers and colonized. By 1948 Britain's control over Palestine was severely compromised by its own state of economic depletion following World War II, and ironically, by the relentless intensity of Zionist terrorist attacks. With mounting international sympathy for Jewish settlement in Palestine, the United Nations proposed a partitioning scheme. In May 1948, a depleted Britain withdrew from a Palestine already descending into civil war. A Jewish state of Israel was declared almost immediately, and was recognized instantly by the United States. Palestinians had been dumped into an abyss of chaos in their own land.

One of the most popular rebellion movements against the British, often recalled with pride by Palestinians, is the Izzedin al-Qassam movement of the 1930s. Sheikh Izzedin al-Qassam was a religious scholar who launched a *Jihad* against the colonial British and their allies, the increasingly militarized European Zionist settlers who by then were flooding Palestine. Decades on, in the early 1990s Hamas's military wing would be named after Sheikh al-Qassam.

When the Zionist intentions became evident of creating a Jewish homeland in Palestine, with the strong support of the European powers, Palestinians tried as early as the beginning of the 1920s to mobilize their Muslim brethren the world over to defend Jerusalem and its holy places. In the year 1938, the first conference to defend *Bait al-Maqdes* was convened in Jerusalem, with delegations from Muslim countries as far distant as Pakistan and Indonesia. Muslim organisations and activities intensified in Palestine in parallel with the increase of activities and the militarization of the Zionist organizations and their settlers.

With the creation of Israel in 1948, a wide shock of humiliation reverberated across the Muslim world. The Jews occupied more than half of Palestine and Jerusalem, and were but a few steps from the al-Aqsa Mosque. The Arabs had been outmanoeuvred by Zionist might and its British collusion. This defeat was astounding, and the disgrace cut deeply into the psyche of Palestinians, Arabs and Muslims. Islam was immediately called upon as an indigenous ideology entrenched throughout Muslim society, which could be used as a rallying point of mobilization in the battle against the enemy and its state as erected in Palestine.

In the 1950s and 1960s Arabs and Palestinians were strongly influenced by nationalist and Marxist ideologies in their campaign to fight Israel and liberate Palestine. As a result, in Palestine and the surrounding countries bordering Israel – Egypt, Syria and Jordan – as well as in more distant countries such as Iraq, Libya and Algeria, Islamist movements were sidelined and Islam as an ideology of mobilization was relegated to the back seat.

Another, and even more mortifying, defeat was looming for the Palestinians and the Arabs in 1967, when Israel launched devastating attacks on Egypt, Syria and Jordan, annexing more land from all of them: Sinai and the Gaza Strip from Egypt, the Golan Heights from Syria and the West Bank with East Jerusalem and the al-Aqsa Mosque from Jordan. With this collapse of the Arab armies, nationalist and Marxist ideologies started to give way to the gradual rise of Islamist movements and political Islam. Starting from the mid-1970s Palestinian Islamists, in the current usage of the word, started establishing stronger footholds in

Palestinian cities. With the victory of the Iranian revolution in the late 1970s, and the defeat of the PLO in Lebanon in 1982, the Palestinian Islamists were steadily on the rise. Their main nationalist rival, the Movement for the Liberation of Palestine (Fatah), had started its long decline. Islam was once again being recalled to the heart of Palestinian politics.

THE MUSLIM BROTHERHOOD ROOTS OF HAMAS

Who are the Muslim Brothers?

In its original thinking and make-up, Hamas belongs to the realm of Muslim Brotherhood movements in the region. These were first established in Egypt in 1928 on the eve of the collapse of the Ottoman Empire. As the major Islamist movement, the Muslim Brotherhood could be considered to be the 'mother of all movements that comprise political Islam' in the Middle East (with the exception of Iran). Over the past eight decades, its branches have been established in almost every Arab country, blending religion and politics to the greatest degree. The Palestinian branch was set up in Jerusalem in 1946, two years before the establishment of the state of Israel.

Although the Muslim Brotherhood was initially mainstream and relatively moderate, many radical small groups have sprouted from it in the last two decades. The influence of its main thinkers, mainly Sayyed Qutob, has had an enormous impact on various strands of political Islam the world over. The main objective of the individual Muslim Brotherhood movements is to establish Islamic states in each of their countries, with the ultimate utopia of uniting individual Islamic states into one single state representing the Muslim *Ummah*.

The Muslim Brotherhood movements, and movements that share the same intellectual background and understanding, are presently the most powerful and active political movements in the Middle East. Robustly represented on the political scene, their members enjoy parliamentary legitimacy or government posts in countries such as Egypt, Jordan, Yemen, Kuwait, Morocco, Algeria, Iraq and Bahrain. They are also strongly represented in the outlawed opposition in places such as Libya, Tunisia, Syria and Saudi Arabia. Although they share the same background and sources of teaching, these movements are greatly coloured by their own nationalist concerns and agenda. There is no obligatory hierarchical organizational structure that combines all of them into one single transnational organization.

Islamist movements, historically and currently, differ greatly in their understanding and interpretation of Islam. In any discussion of the Hamas movement, the two major issues that need to be distinguished are the differing perceptions of various Islamist movements concerning the 'ends' versus the 'means'. The 'ends' issue denotes the extent to which politics is ingrained in Islam, whereas the 'means' issue reflects the controversy on the use of violence to achieve the 'ends'. The spectrum of such interpretations tends to vacillate between two extremes. At one end there is an understanding of Islam that politicizes religion and renders it the ultimate judge in all aspects of life, including politics. At the other end, there is a different interpretation and an apolitical understanding of Islam, where it is argued that efforts should be focused on morals and religious teachings, away from politics and state-making, and where the sole accepted ways of conveying the word of Islam are peaceful ones.

Along the spectrum of Islamist movements, the Muslim Brotherhood occupies almost the centre of the continuum in terms of 'ends' and 'means'. The Muslim Brotherhood believes in politicized religion and religious politics, hence its strong conviction that Islamic states must be established. It became established that the means to realize this end were undoubtedly peaceful, as had been stressed by the movement's founders back in the Egypt of the 1930s. Yet over the following decades, groups within the Muslim Brotherhood adopted violence and clashed with governments in

Egypt and Syria. Since the mid-1980s they have overwhelmingly adhered to peaceful means, even when confronted with extreme oppressive measures, as was the case with the Tunisian Islamist movement in the late 1980s and afterwards.

On one side of the Muslim Brotherhood's centre position on this ends/means continuum, there are groups such as al-Qaeda which embrace violence wholeheartedly in their pursuit of their political aims. Hamas also lies somewhere on this side of the continuum, but closer to the Muslim Brotherhood than to al-Qaeda, by virtue of its unique specificity of using violence only against foreign occupying powers and not against legitimate national governments. On the other side of the Muslim Brotherhood there are groups that distance themselves from politics, such as al-Dawa wal Tabligh, which believes only in spreading religious teaching and morality, and Hizb al-Tahrir, whose politicization of religion is perhaps stronger than that of the Muslim Brotherhood, but it believes neither in violence nor in political participation in existing systems. The fight for it is purely intellectual.

What are the links between the Muslim Brotherhood, Palestine and Hamas?

Hamas represents the internal metamorphosis of the Palestinian Muslim Brotherhoods which took place in the late 1980s. Officially, the Palestinian branch of the Muslim Brotherhood was founded in 1946 in Jerusalem, although its presence and activities in Palestine go back to 1943/44 in Gaza City, Jerusalem, Nablus and other cities. The aims, structure and outlook of the Palestinian Muslim Brotherhood were drawn along the main lines of thinking of the mother organization in Egypt, where Islamization of society is the prime goal. At this time there was no Israel, and Islamists were simply dealing with the British mandate and the growing power of the Zionist movement.

There is no record of the Palestinian Muslim Brotherhood

fighting against British troops in Palestine during the mandate period. The Egyptian Muslim Brotherhood, however, took part in the 1948 war against the British by sending hundreds of volunteers to fight alongside the then-weak Egyptian army. After the creation of the state of Israel in 1948, the Palestinian Muslim Brotherhood was physically divided into two parts; one in the West Bank which was annexed to Jordan and where the Palestinian Muslim Brotherhood joined the Jordanian Branch of the Muslim Brotherhood, and one in the Gaza Strip, which was left under Egyptian administration, and thus the Palestinian Muslim Brotherhood there became close to the Egyptian Muslim Brotherhood.

By the war of 1967 new political and geographical realities were brought into being when the entire area of historic Palestine, including the West Bank and the Gaza Strip, fell under Israeli control. The two wings of the Palestinian Muslim Brotherhood, the Gazan and the West Bank, became closer and developed unitary structures over the years. In the 1970s and 1980s, the Palestinian Muslim Brotherhood amassed strength and established footholds in all major Palestinian cities. On the broader Palestinian political scene, leftist and nationalist movements had been outpacing and outpowering the Muslim Brotherhood in both Gaza and the West Bank from as early as the 1940s up to the late 1980s. In particular, the Fatah movement (the Palestinian National Movement for the Liberation of Palestine), and the PLO (the Palestine Liberation Organization) which is the wider umbrella of the national Palestinian movements, dominated Palestinian politics over those decades.

The 1980s witnessed a rapid growth in the power of the Muslim Brotherhood. In December 1987 a popular Palestinian uprising, the *intifada*, against the Israeli occupation erupted first in the Gaza Strip, then in the West Bank. On the eve of that uprising, the Palestinian Muslim Brotherhood decided to undertake a major transformation within the movement. It established Hamas as an adjunct organisation with the specific mission of confronting the Israeli occupation.

Are there other Islamist movements in Palestine?

There have been, and still are, Islamist movements other than Hamas in Palestine. The most important one is the Islamic Jihad Movement, established in early 1980s, at least five years before the emergence of Hamas. The Islamic Jihad was formed by discontented former members of both the Muslim Brotherhoods, Fatah and other nationalist and leftist Palestinian factions. Inspired by the victory of the Islamic revolution in Iran in 1978/9, the idea of the Islamic Jihad was to form a bridge between Islam and Palestine, which were separately represented by the Muslim Brotherhood on the one hand, and the nationalist camp (the PLO) on the other hand.

When the Palestinian Muslim Brotherhood, the mother organization of Hamas, was immersed in its religious programmes in the first years of 1980s, the Islamic Jihad offered a new version of nationalist Islam which incorporated the struggle against Israel into the very heart of Islamic discourse and practice. Between 1982 and 1987, the Islamic Jihad posed a serious challenge to the Muslim Brotherhood because of its adoption of military resistance against the occupation. It also posed an equal challenge to the nationalist factions whose main criticism of the Muslim Brotherhood concerned its deferment of confrontation with the Israeli occupation. If the PLO was nationalist enough, but lacked an Islamic dimension, and if the Palestinian MB was Islamist enough, but lacked a nationalist dimension, the Islamic Jihad combined both components and had ended what it had seen to be a disconnection between Islam and Palestine.

In the second half of the 1990s, and during the second Palestinian uprising in the year 2000, the Islamic Jihad carried out many suicide attacks. At certain periods, it outpaced Hamas and other factions in this practice. However, the Islamic Jihad is weak in its membership and networking, and this is why it shows little enthusiasm for elections. Its justification is that elections absorb national energy that should be directed toward resisting the Israelis. In the 1990s whenever the Islamic Jihad took part in even minor elections for student unions or trade unions, its results ranged between 4 and 7 per cent compared with 45 to 55 per cent for Hamas.

Another Islamist movement with a certain visible presence in Palestine, if with less current relevance, is Hizb al-Tahrir (the Liberation Party). It was founded in 1952 as a splinter group of the Muslim Brotherhood. Its main belief is that the source of all sins in Muslim societies is the disappearance of Khilafa, the overarching Muslim rule, and that all efforts should be focused on restoring Khilafa. Once in power, the Khalifa (the person representing the supreme Islamic authority) can mobilize Muslims by virtue of his appeal, and his power if necessary, and direct them to work for any cause. The failure of Muslims (including Palestinians), Hizb al-Tahrir concludes, stems from their overlooking this premise. Grassroots efforts and gradual Islamization are fruitless. Change should be undertaken from above, and when the Khalifa is in power, many problems that face Muslims will be solved. Regarding the Palestinian question and confronting the Israeli occupation, Hizb al-Tahrir maintains a passive approach which has lost it popularity and leverage among Palestinians. The party opposes all forms of political participation, such as elections, and, in the absence of the Khalifa, it opposes a resort to violence against either national governments or Israel.

THE FORMATION OF HAMAS

When, why and how was Hamas founded?

Hamas came into being officially on 14 December 1987, declaring itself in an official communiqué a few days after the eruption of the first *intifada*, the Palestinian uprising, on 8 December. The decision to establish the Islamic Resistance Movement (Hamas) was taken on the day following the *intifada* by top leaders of the Palestinian Muslim Brothers, Sheikh Ahmad Yasin, Abdul 'Aziz al-Rantisi, Salah Shehadeh, Muhammad Sham'ah, 'Isa al-Nashar,

'Abdul Fattah Dukhan and Ibrahim al-Yazuri. (The first three were assassinated by Israel in later years.)

Hamas was formed by the Palestinian Muslim Brotherhood itself in order to respond to a number of factors pressing upon the organization. Internally and by the time of the *intifada*, the rank and file of the Palestinian Muslim Brotherhood were witnessing intense internal debate on the passive approach to the Israeli occupation. There were two opposing views. One pushed for a change in policy toward confrontation with the occupation, thus bypassing old and traditional thinking whose focus was on the Islamization of society first. The other view clung to the classical school of thought within the Muslim Brotherhood movements, which adhered to the concept of 'preparing the generations for a battle' which had no deadline. When the *intifada* erupted, the exponents of the confrontational policy gained a stronger position, arguing that Islamists would suffer a great loss if they decided not to take part in the *intifada*, definitively and equally with all the other participating Palestinian factions.

Externally, hard living conditions for Palestinians in the Gaza Strip, which had been created and exacerbated by the Israeli occupation, reached an unprecedented state. Poverty combined with feelings of oppression and humiliation charged the Palestinian atmosphere with the ripe conditions for revolt against the occupation. The *intifada* was the flashpoint. The explosion reflected the accumulation of past experiences and suffering more than any specific event that triggered things on the first day of the uprising. Strategically speaking, it was the golden opportunity for the Palestinian Muslim Brotherhood to heed (and be seen to lead) the uprising. It did just so by creating Hamas.

Externally there was the factor of the rivalry at this time from a similar Islamic organization, not as national or leftist as the Islamic Jihad. As discussed above, the Islamic Jihad Movement had been on the rise during the few years preceding the *intifada*. The very incident that triggered the *intifada* itself involved Islamic Jihad members who freed themselves from an

Israeli prison and engaged in a shoot-out with the Israeli soldiers. Feeling envious of the Islamic Jihad and its members, who emerged as heroes in the eyes of the Palestinians after the incident, the Palestinian Muslim Brotherhood felt the danger of losing ground to its small, yet more active, competitor. The presence and activities of the Islamic Jihad partly compelled the Muslim Brotherhood to speed up its internal transformation.

Why did the Palestinian Islamists only start their armed struggle against Israeli occupation in 1987 when this occupation started in 1967?

In the thinking of the Muslim Brothers, both in Palestine prior to the creation of Hamas and in other countries, the failures of Muslims – their backwardness, weakness and their defeat by their enemies – were the results of their deviation from the true path of Islam. Therefore, the proper process for redressing all of these failures, including the defeat in the wars against Israel, was first to educate Muslims about Islam and make them committed to their religion. Transforming people from ignorant Muslims into adherents would rehabilitate all of Muslim society and prepare it for the fight with its enemies, from the certainty of standing on strong ground. In the rhetoric of the Muslim Brotherhood this was called 'preparing the generations'.

The Palestinian Muslim Brothers had a deep conviction in this principle, which they consistently used to justify their non-confrontation policy against the Israeli occupation during the 1950s, 1960s, 1970s and until 1987. Against mounting accusations by other Palestinian nationalist and leftist organisations of cowardice or even of being indirectly in the service of the Israeli occupation, the Palestinian Islamists clung to their strategy of 'preparing the generations' for a long time. They argued that it was a fruitless effort to fight Israel with a 'corrupt army'; instead one should build a devoted and religiously committed army, then engage in war against Israel.

This strategy came under continuous attack. For Palestinian nationalists and leftists, such an approach was a mere justification for refraining from joining the national struggle. It was also criticized as naive on two levels, the first being the association of an individual's capacity and genuine intention to fight the occupation with his or her level of religious commitment, and the second being the contrast between the open-ended abstraction of 'preparing the generations' with the daily imperative of engagement with the enemy. The true preparation of people to fight for their national rights and liberation, critics argued, is to fully engage in the struggle, where people learn and empower themselves as they advance and suffer. Moreover, Israel was understandably happy with the Islamists' concept of 'delaying the struggle' until the Palestinian generations were spiritually and morally well prepared and ready.

Hamas's supporters retrospectively defend the earlier thinking of their mother organization. They say that it was just exactly this strategy that guaranteed a strong beginning for Hamas and its continuous achievements on the ground in the years which followed. For them, the need for gradual and patient preparation was actually justified because in the 1960s and 1970s the Islamists were militarily very weak, and had they involved themselves in fruitless confrontation against Israel then, they would have been crushed easily, serving neither Palestine nor Islam.

Regardless of their rationalizations, the Islamists paid a high price during the decades when they opted for a non-confrontational policy. They provided the opportunity for their national rivals to outpace them, and put themselves in a disadvantageous position. More importantly, they deprived the Palestinian struggle against the Israeli occupation of the participation and contribution of that significant segment of the Palestinian population who came under the influence of the Palestinian Muslim Brotherhood and its thinking.

2 Hamas's ideology, strategy and objectives

THE DEFINITION OF HAMAS, ITS IDEOLOGICAL DRIVE AND WORLDVIEW

What is Hamas, and is it driven by religious or political convictions?

Perhaps the most informative answer to this common question can be found in a lengthy self-definition that Hamas once produced by way of introducing itself to a European government, years prior to its assuming power in 2006. In this self-definition, Hamas states its aims and strategies in addition to its long-term view for the solution in Palestine. Hamas describes itself as follows:

> The Islamic Resistance Movement (Hamas) is a Palestinian national liberation movement that struggles for the liberation of the Palestinian occupied territories and for the recognition of the legitimate rights of Palestinians. Although it came into existence soon after the eruption of the first Palestinian intifadah (uprising) in December 1987 as an expression of the Palestinian people's anger against the continuation of the Israeli occupation of Palestinian land and persecution of the Palestinian people, Hamas' roots extend much deeper in history.

The movement's motivation for resistance has been expressed by its founder and leader Sheikh Ahmad Yassin: 'The movement struggles against Israel because it is the aggressing, usurping and oppressing state that day and night hoists the rifle in the face of our sons and daughters.'

Hamas considers itself to be an extension of an old tradition that goes back to the early twentieth century struggle against British and Zionist colonialism in Palestine. The fundamentals from which it derives its legitimacy are mirrored in the very name it chose for itself. Hamas, in the Islamic language, means that it derives its guiding principles from the doctrines and values of Islam. Islam is completely Hamas' ideological frame of reference. It is from the values of Islam that the movement seeks its inspiration in its mobilisation effort, and particularly in seeking to address the huge difference in material resources between the Palestinian people and their supporters on the one hand and Israel and its supporters on the other. ...

The forms of resistance adopted by Hamas stem from the same justifications upon which the national Palestinian resistance movement has based its struggle for more than a quarter of a century. At least the first ten articles of the Palestinian National Charter issued by the PLO show complete compatibility with Hamas' discourse as elaborated in its Charter and other declarations. Furthermore, the same justifications for resistance had, prior to the emergence of Hamas in December 1987, been recognised, or endorsed, by a variety of regional and international bodies such as the Arab League, the Islamic Conference Organisation, the Non-Aligned Movement and the United Nations. It is clearly recognised that the

Israeli occupation of the West Bank and Gaza in 1967 is illegal in UN Security Council Resolutions 242 and 338. ...

In spite of the overwhelming militant image it has in the minds of many people in the West, Hamas is not a mere military faction. It is a political, cultural and social grass roots organisation that has a separate military wing specialising in armed resistance against Israeli occupation. Apart from this strategically secretive military wing, all other sections within Hamas function through overt public platforms. The military wing has its own leadership and recruiting mechanism.

Hamas's social and educational activities in the Occupied Territories have become so interwoven within the Palestinian community that neither the Israelis nor their peace partners in the Palestinian Authority have been able to extricate them one from the other. The fact of the matter is that Hamas, contrary to Israeli assessment, acts as an infrastructure to the numerous cultural, educational and social institutions in Gaza and the West Bank that render invaluable and irreplaceable services to the public. In other words, it is Hamas that gives life to these institutions and not the reverse. The Israelis have repeatedly told the PA to close them down. The PA has tried but failed. A crackdown on these institutions amounts to a declaration of war not against Hamas but against the Palestinian community as a whole.

It must be pointed out that the above text identifies Hamas with the Palestinians' struggle to liberate their land only. There is no implication, either explicit or tacit, of any intention to establish an Islamic state in Palestine in the future, or any similar goals advocated by other Islamist organizations. There is further discussion of this below.

What is Hamas's ultimate aim? Is it to establish an Islamic state in Palestine?

The vague idea of establishing an Islamic state in Palestine as mentioned in the early statements of the movement was quickly sidelined and surpassed. Even when it was repeated by members of Hamas it never amounted to any really serious proposal with thoughtfully considered details. If anything, its early reluctant existence, followed by almost complete disappearance in Hamas's documentation and discourse, reflected the tension in the minds of Hamas's leaders between the political and the religious. On one hand there is the subconscious urge to remain sincere to the pure pre-Hamas religious utopia where the dream of an Islamic state sought to fulfil the goals of the long-distant future. On the other hand, the oversimplification and naivety of this dream exposed the extent to which Hamas needed to become aware of the realities of what the Palestinians were dealing with, on the ground, day after day. In this light, the Hamas dream of a pure Islamic state was practically embarrassing, but the realization of this developed a more sophisticated Hamas, a Hamas content to look towards the actual needs of a Palestinian people under siege.

Palestinians across the spectrum of political convictions have struggled desperately for more than eight decades to extract even minimal legitimate rights, first from British occupiers following the 1922 Mandate, in which Britain was apportioned control of the part of the former Ottoman Empire that included Palestine, and then from 1948, when Britain withdrew from Palestine, leaving the Zionist organization to declare the Jewish state of Israel, with the Israeli government. That government has essentially been occupying and colonizing not only those parts of Palestine 'allocated' to it by the UN 1947 division plan, but even large areas of Palestine that were not. After all these decades of struggle, the maximum that the Palestinian leadership has struggled to achieve, without success, has been the retention or recovery of no more than one-eighth of the historic land of Palestine.

The Islamic state put forth in early Hamas literature was visualized to include the whole of Palestine from the River Jordan to the Mediterranean Sea. The question became, would Hamas wait in hope for full liberation of all historic Palestine, or would it seek to impose a temporary Islamic state in just the West Bank and the Gaza Strip if they were ever returned to the Palestinians? What kind of state would this be, and how would it deal with its surroundings, with Israel, with the world? On what basis would it do so? And so forth. There was a list of endless intractable questions surrounded this idea of establishing an Islamic state, and eventually it ended in complete trivialization, with Hamas dropping the idea altogether.

If not the formation of an Islamic state, then what now is Hamas's ultimate goal? A plain answer, suggested by the movement's formal declarations, might be the simple total liberation of the historic land of Palestine from the River Jordan to the Mediterranean Sea. However, similar to the utopian religious goal of establishing an Islamic state, this utopian nationalist goal tends to be mentioned less and less in Hamas's documents and verbal statements. In fact, the longer Hamas functions, the less interest it shows in adopting or declaring 'ultimate goals'. Hamas has developed, and is still developing, into a movement that is more and more preoccupied with current and immediate, and medium-term, goals.

In the course of taking power after the elections of 2006, Hamas has focused its pre and post-elections discourse on the concept of explicitly resisting the illegal Israeli occupation while implicitly if reluctantly accepting the principle of a two-state solution. Neither an Islamic state nor the total liberation of Palestine have been emphasized. The ultimate goals, thus, have been replaced with short and medium-term ones, more pressing and more realistic.

What is Hamas's strategy?

To confirm its move out of the realm of far-fetched dreams,
Hamas started to advocate more achievable goals in both the short
and medium term. It not only sought immediate relief and benefits for Palestinians on the ground now, it pursued goals that could
be comprehended by regional and international audiences. Mini-
mizing the religious in its use of language, Hamas's discourse has
became more aware, embracing legal jargon and basing itself on
the norms of international law. Yet Hamas still struggles to keep
alive the principle of the 'liberation of Palestine' as a whole, in the
mildest way possible, within the context of the immediate challenges faced by the movement and Palestinians at large. In the
few years after the first *intifada* Hamas developed its strategy
considerably from the initial raw statements mentioned in its
charter. In 1993 it issued an 'Introductory Memorandum'. Under
the heading 'The Movement's Strategy', it read:

> Hamas constructs its strategy for confronting the
> Zionist occupation as follows:
> - The Palestinian people, being the primary target of
>   the occupation, bear the larger part of the burden in
>   resisting it. Hamas, therefore, works to mobilize the
>   energies of these people and to direct them toward
>   steadfastness.
> - The field of engagement with the enemy is Palestine,
>   Arab and Islamic lands being fields of aid and
>   support to our people, especially those lands that
>   have been enriched with the pure blood of [Islamic]
>   martyrs throughout the ages.
> - Confronting and resisting the enemy in Palestine
>   must be continuous until victory and liberation. Holy
>   struggle in the name of God as our guide, and fight-
>   ing and inflicting harm on enemy troops and their
>   instruments rank at the top of our means of resistance.
> - Political activity, in our view, is one means of holy

struggle against the Zionist enemy and aims to buttress the struggle and steadfastness of our people and to mobilize its energies and that of our Arab Islamic nation to render our cause victorious.

In this strategy Hamas confirms the 'boundaries' of the armed conflict, stating clearly that it wishes to undertake no military steps outside Palestine: 'the field of engagement with the enemy is Palestine'. Hamas reiterates this conviction in its strategy to assure the outside world that attacking any western or even Israeli targets outside Palestine is not on the agenda of the movement.

It is worth mentioning that these guidelines were outlined 13 years before Hamas came to power and took control of the Palestinian Authority in January 2006. These broad proclamations of Hamas's strategy were drawn with very little expectation, if any, of where political and military developments concerning the Israeli–Palestinian conflict would lead the Palestinians. Surely it was beyond the imagination of the people who drafted the above strategy that Hamas would one day be allowed to win free and fair democratic elections to control a limited self-rule authority created according to peace agreements between Hamas's rivals and Israel.

This new situation has brought the cornerstone of Hamas's strategy – 'military resistance' to the Israeli occupation – under close scrutiny. In taking over a government of besieged and weakened authority, Hamas was overwhelmed by the numerous issues relating to the simple daily living of Palestinians. Any thought of military resistance appeared for a while to be a luxury that the movement could not afford. As was noted above, Hamas had pragmatically recognized earlier that the immediate welfare of the besieged Palestinian people was as important as any more long-term ideological ideals. It has managed to save face as the party of resistance by adopting the standard line that 'political activity … is itself one of the means of struggle', a line echoed in the statement often made by its leaders that military resistance is not an end in itself, but a means to an end. Thus, being consumed in government undertakings and serving the Palestinian people on a daily basis can easily be linked to the broad parameters of resistance.

How does Hamas perceive the world?

Hamas's immediate world, as explained in its literature, comprises three concentric circles: the Palestinian core, the larger Arabic circle and the larger still embracing Islamic circle. Beyond those circles lies the rest of the world. The question of Palestine is, for Hamas, the fundamental determinant in shaping the relationship between those three circles and the rest of the world. The movement's literature states that:

> Hamas believes that the ongoing conflict between Arabs and Muslims and Zionists in Palestine is a fateful civilizational struggle incapable of being brought to an end without eliminating its cause, namely, the Zionist settlement of Palestine.

The West is charged not only with the responsibility of having illegally created Israel but also with bringing devastation and dismemberment to the region as a whole:

> This enterprise of aggression [on Palestine] complements the larger Western project that seeks to strip this Arab Islamic nation of its cultural roots in order to consolidate Western Zionist hegemony over it by completing the plan of greater Israel and establishing political and economic control of it. Doing so implies maintaining the [current] state of [physical] division, backwardness, and dependency in which this Arab Islamic nation is forced to live. The conflict as described is a form of struggle between truth and falsehood, which obligates Arabs and Muslims to support the Palestinians in bearing the consequences

of a holy struggle to extirpate the Zionist presence from Palestine and prevent it from spreading to other Arab and Islamic countries.

Of the circles surrounding Palestine, the first one is Arabic, the second is Islamic and the third is the rest of the world. Naturally more affinity and intimacy is felt towards the closer Arabic and Islamic circles. There is a considerable amount of dismay, criticism and attack against the indifference that the outermost circle comprising the 'world' has exhibited concerning the suffering of the Palestinians. The western world is typically criticized and accused not only of 'transplanting' Israel in Palestine – at the heart of the Arab region – by force, but also for its continuous support of the 'usurping and aggressive Zionist state' which has sought even to exceed the borders of the original illegal foundation.

In its very early stages, Hamas thinking was skewed by a dichotomy that bisected the world into the 'truthfulness' represented by Muslims and believers, and the 'falsehood' represented by non-Muslims and particularly westerners and Jews. This naïve perception later almost disappeared from the movement's discourses. In tandem with Hamas's rise in influence, the expansion of its regional and international relations and its realization of the complexity of reality and politics at ground level, Hamas has rehabilitated its 'worldview' and effectively abandoned the dichotomy based on believers/nonbelievers. The notion of political support for the Palestinians and their just cause has prevailed as the defining parameter by which Hamas assesses world players and where they stand.

WHAT IS THE HAMAS CHARTER, AND IS IT RELEVANT?

Published in August 1988, nine months after the emergence of Hamas, the 'Charter' is one of the first basic documents that was published with the aim of introducing the new movement first to its immediate, then to broader, constituencies. It was meant to be the founding treatise: the embodiment of Hamas's objectives, vision and beliefs, and the movement's guideline for its strategy and worldview. The main emphasis of the Charter is to assert that Palestine is an Arab and Muslim land that should be liberated from Zionist domination, and that Israel is a 'usurper' and an alien entity which was 'transplanted' in Palestine only with the support of Western superpowers. Ironically, the Charter failed to maintain a central position in Hamas's political thinking; a few years after its publication it was shunted onto the margins with little reference to its content. It was deemed by many Hamas leaders both inside and outside Palestine to be simplistic and overloaded with claims and arguments that would reflect a naïve, rather than a sophisticated, image of Hamas. In several interviews over the years I have been told by a number of Hamas leaders that the Charter was written by one leading personality in the Gaza Strip, and distributed hastily without enough prior consultation.

The Charter is a long document which in English runs to 24 pages,[1] and consists of five chapters with 36 articles which tackle a wide array of issues and positions. The general language of the Charter is distinctively polemic and characteristically religious, unlike the more politically nuanced language that Hamas has adopted in subsequent years. All the chapters are infused with Quranic verses, Hadiths, quotations from prominent religious people, ancient and contemporary, and sometime classical Arab poetry. A considerable measure of obscurity and a generic Islamic bent in the Charter has

---

1 For the full text of the English-translated version see Khaled Hroub, *Hamas: Political Thought and Practice* (Washington DC: Institute of Palestine Studies, 2000), pp. 267–91, from which all the quotations and references from the charter in this section are taken.

produced a de-Palestinized discourse, which makes it less easy to understand the specifics or relevance of certain statements or discursive engagement in the text. 'Modern' references are also made especially to European anti-Semitic discourse blaming the Jews for all the sins and catastrophes in the world.

In its introduction the Charter is introduced as follows:

> This is the Charter of the Islamic Resistance Movement (Hamas), showing its form, revealing its identity, stating its position, clarifying its expectations, discussing its hopes, and calling for aid, support, and a joining of its ranks, because our struggle with the Jews is long and dangerous, requiring all dedicated efforts. It is a phase that must be followed by succeeding phases, a battalion that must be supported by battalion after battalion of the vast Arab and Islamic world until the enemy is defeated and the victory of God prevails.

The first chapter of the Charter is the 'Introduction of the movement' where the text is anxious to declare that Hamas is 'a branch of the Muslim Brotherhood chapter in Palestine', emphasizing that the 'Islamic perspective' of the Brothers is the same as that of Hamas. This chapter goes on to outline the 'structure and essence' of Hamas, where little but general abstractions is given, such as 'The structure of Hamas is comprised of Muslims who are devoted to God and worship Him verily'; 'The historical and geographical dimensions of the Islamic resistance movement', where Islam is confirmed as the 'origin' of the movement and where its geography 'extends to wherever Muslims are found'. In the sections 'Differentiation and independence' and the 'Universality of the Islamic resistance movement' the first signs of bold 'Palestinianism' emerge in the Charter, which states that Hamas is 'a distinct Palestinian movement', similar in some ways to but different in others from other movements.

Chapter 2, the shortest in the Charter, deals with Objectives, and stipulates that:

> The goal of Hamas ... is to conquer evil, crushing it and defeating it, so that truth may prevail, so that the country may return to its rightful place, and so that the call may be heard from the minarets proclaiming the Islamic state. And aid is sought from God.

Achieving this goal is described in Chapter 3, the longest in the Charter, through 'Strategies and methods'. The opening statement of this chapter affirms that:

> The Islamic resistance movement believes that the land of Palestine is an Islamic land entrusted to the Muslim generations until Judgement Day. No one may renounce all or even part of it. No Arab state nor all Arab states combined, no king or president nor all kings and presidents, and no organization nor all organizations, Palestinian or Arab, have the right to dispose of it or relinquish or cede any part of it.

The chapter moves on to discuss 'Nation and nationalism from the point of view of the Islamic resistance movement', considering nationalism as 'part and parcel of religious ideology'. Then it emphasizes the role of *jihad* in fighting the occupiers: 'If an enemy invades Muslim territories then Jihad and fighting the enemy becomes an individual duty on every Muslim.' *Jihad* is the only way to restore rights: 'There is no solution to the Palestinian problem except through struggle [*jihad*]. As for international initiatives and conferences, they are a waste of time, a kind of child's play.'

Further 'strategies' are laid down by elaborating the 'three circles' that should be engaged in the liberation of Palestine: 'the Palestinian circle; the Arab circle; and the Islamic circle', each of which has its contribution to the 'battle'. In order to prepare the Palestinians and other Muslims to engage in this battle, a process of 'Islamic education and training' should be undertaken, as the text points out, where the 'role of Muslim women', the 'role of Islamic art in the battle of liberation' and 'social solidarity' are given specific attention.

Perhaps the most embarrassing part of the entire Charter in the eyes of today's Hamas is the less-than-one-page section under the title 'Forces abetting the enemy'. Here the Charter paints a picture of the 'global conspiracy' that was behind the establishment of Israel. It states:

> The enemies have planned well to get where they are, taking into account the effective measures in current affairs ... with money they financed revolutions throughout the world in pursuit of their objectives. They were behind the French Revolution, the Communist Revolution, and most of the revolutions here and there that we heard about and are hearing of. With wealth they established clandestine organizations all over the world, such as the Freemasons, the Rotary and Lions Clubs, etc., to destroy societies and promote the interests of Zionism. These are all destructive intelligence-gathering organizations ... let us speak without hesitation: They were behind the First World War in which they destroyed the Islamic Caliphate ... monopolized the wealth and got the Balfour Declaration. They created the League of Nations through which they could rule the world. They were behind the Second World War .... There was no war that broke out anywhere without their hands behind it.

Chapter 4, 'Our position', is devoted to Hamas's positions regarding a number of immediate and pressing issues (and parties). It starts by offering amicable gestures toward 'Other Islamic movements' (hinting at Hizb al-Tahrir in Palestine and the Islamic Jihad Movement; the latter was amassing popularity to a degree considered 'alarming' by the Palestinian Muslim Brotherhood at the time of the emergence of Hamas). Then the text outlines Hamas's position regarding 'patriotic (secular) movements in the Palestinian arena', confirming that it will 'lend its support to them as long as they do not give loyalty either to the communist East or the crusading West'. Regarding Hamas's relationship with the PLO however, the Charter attempts to carefully describe a position that shows appreciation of the organization, but remains far from acknowledging it as the representative of the Palestinian people, using the excuse of the secular nature of the PLO: 'despite our respect for the Palestine Liberation Organization and what it might become, and not reducing its role in the Arab–Israeli struggle, we cannot exchange the Islamic nature of Palestine for the secular ideology [of the PLO]'.

Chapter 5, which is a short conclusion, is meant to inject hope and steadfastness into Hamas's followers by means of citing the 'Historical proof: facing the enemy throughout history', as the title of the chapter goes. Here the text reaches another peak in its polemics, declaring that 'Palestine is the heart of the earth, the meeting of the continents, the object of greed for the avaricious since the dawn of history'. Then it refers to the current 'Zionist invasion of Palestine' as a passing phase that will only follow previous failed phases:

> The current Zionist invasion has been preceded by the many invasions of the crusading West and others, such as the Tartars from the East. The Muslims confronted those invasions, prepared for fighting, and defeated them. They should be able to confront and defeat the Zionist invasion.

Now that I have outlined the main themes addressed in the Hamas Charter, it is important however to reiterate that the significance that is given to the Charter in much anti-Hamas literature is in fact unjustified. Also, the often-repeated charges that the Charter explicitly calls for the 'destruction of Israel' or the 'termination of the Jews' are not accurate; no such literal phrases occur in the Charter. There is no doubt, however, that the Charter with its rhetoric and unlimited generalizations has inflicted much damage upon Hamas. But the movement's literature since 1990 has become far more sophisticated than what was initially presented in the Charter (see Chapter 10). As explained elsewhere in this book, Hamas's more current discourse is politically driven, unlike the Charter's heavily religiously riddled language. To change or replace the Charter, however, would be a very difficult and delicate step, and it is one that Hamas has lacked the courage to take. Hamas leaders fear that such a step would be construed by many as giving up on the basic principles of the movement. What Hamas has resigned itself to do, thus far, is to let the Charter die on its own, moving on and leaving it behind; hoping it will just go away. Yet the cost of simply downplaying its existence remains high, as all that is stated in the Charter is still formally taken to be representative of Hamas.

HAMAS: A NATIONAL LIBERATION MOVEMENT OR A RELIGIOUS MOVEMENT?

What are the nationalist elements and religious elements in Hamas's thinking and practice?

Hamas is a blend of national liberation movement and Islamist religious group. By virtue of such a nature its driving forces are dual, its daily functioning is biaxial and its end goals are bifocal, where each side of each binary serves the other.

The dual driving reasons for Palestinians to join Hamas are to actively engage in the 'liberation of Palestine' by resisting the Israeli occupation and whatever else that may take, *and* to serve

Islam and spread its word. The word 'and' is pivotal here and cannot be replaced by the word 'or', though the balance between the two motives need not be equal or the same in everyone. Hamas considers that its power is to be found in this link, the strengthened alloy of these two separate strands of Palestinian political activism: the national secular liberation movement that has confronted Israel, *and* the Islamist religious movement that largely has not. The desired thinking is that in struggling for the liberation of Palestine, an individual is serving Islam, and in strengthening the call of Islam this individual serves the liberation struggle.

In fact, this is one of the major underlying reasons explaining the continuous rise of Hamas. People with strong nationalist feelings and the drive to struggle against Israel, and with a traditional Islamist background, tend to choose Hamas as their natural movement. Others, with strong religious sentiments and who also want to be active against Israel, also join Hamas. Indeed, it is to be expected that both driving forces will occupy the mind and soul of the Hamas membership, but certainly their strengths differ at the level of individuals. For example, members of the Muslim Brotherhood organization who became de facto members of Hamas when the former was transformed into the latter tend to nurture a stronger religious drive than those members who joined Hamas in later stages and defected from other nationalist factions.

The day-to-day operations of Hamas are therefore spread along the axis of religious and nationalist activities. It devotes considerable efforts to educating its membership according to Islamic ideals, as understood and interpreted by the organization. Mainly by using mosques, Hamas has built a strong generation of young people who are adherents of Islam. From committed daily prayers and reciting Quranic verses to fighting 'vice' in the street, Hamas members adhere to the finest details of Islamic rituals. The other part of the daily function of Hamas is the struggle against Israel. It is deeply believed in Hamas's thinking that the more devout the individual is, the more self-sacrificing on the battlefield he or she will be. In this way, religious teaching strengthens the liberation front.

The ultimate goals of Hamas are also dual: the 'liberation of Palestine' and the Islamization of society (or the establish-ment of an Islamic state). In the early Hamas thinking and among rigid Palestinian Islamists, these two goals can never be reached simultaneously, but must come in sequence. For them, it would be futile to try to liberate Palestine before achieving a satisfactory degree of Islamization in Palestinian society. To their way of thinking, only religious and Islam-disciplined indi-viduals would be able to defeat Israel. What Hamas has done within that traditional thinking is to break the imagined sequence and argue that both processes can be fought for in parallel. In this, Hamas attracts both those who want to liberate Palestine, and those who want to Islamize Palestinian society.

How far are the nationalists and the religious reconciled within Hamas?

During Hamas's lifetime, the movement has shown a reasonable degree of reconciliation between its nationalist and religious sides. This was helped by the fact that it was in opposition until recently, and never faced the really challenging practical contradictions that arise in the actual practice of governance.

From the nationalist perspective, in the religious aspect of the movement Hamas had mixed fortunes. It maintained extraordinary discipline and a high level of sacrifice from the movement's rank and file with regard to the struggle against Israel. This was the basis for the movement's social solidarity work, which benefited wider Palestinian constituencies, espe-cially in the face of extreme hardship and poverty in refugee camps and deprived areas. Yet at the same time the religious aspect has sometimes taken over the political and nationalist aspect of Hamas at the grassroots level. The major controversial religious practice that Hamas has adopted, directly or indirectly, is the perceived imposition of religious moral codes on Palestinians. In parallel to its rise in influence a quasi-intimidating atmosphere was created particularly in the Gaza Strip, where people felt indirect pressure to comply with Hamas's dictates on moral issues. This issue is discussed in detail in Chapter 5, but the relevant point here is that moves to the forced Islamization of society provoked anger and condemnation among some, at the expense of Hamas's nationalist appeal.

From the religious perspective, the nationalist aspect of the movement also brought Hamas mixed fortunes. In the first place it gave Palestinian Islamists an immensely needed legitimacy, which originated in the mere fact that they were confronting the Israeli occupation. Thus the Palestinian Islamist movement, in its new transformation as Hamas, became bestowed with an additional appeal to reach out to more potential followers and recruits. Moreover, the heavier involvement in the nationalist confrontational effort has broadened the perspectives and experiences of Palestinian Islamists, and brought them to the fore of political realities. This of course propelled the movement to mesh its religious understanding, by way of issuing *fatwas* – religious justifications of successive political and even pseudo-military actions – with the rapid pace of the nationalist struggle and its political requirements. However, the nationalist element was seen as sometimes and in certain ways preaching to or overriding the province of the religious. This has taken place under the surface, in areas such as striking alliances with leftist groups, and participation in politically concerted efforts that could involve agreeing politically on matters that would be disapproved of from the religious viewpoint. For example, in 1996 Hamas boycotted the elections for the legislative council, but in 2006 it not only participated in the elections, it won them. This change faced some internal religious disapproval. A minority of voices considered these elections to be *haram* (forbidden) because they involved a compromise over the 'Islamic land of Palestine and Islamic sovereignty over it'.

In summary, Hamas managed to keep its nationalist and religious components somewhat harmonious before taking power in the year 2006. In the post-election era and with Hamas in power, the tension between the religious and the nationalist/ political dimensions within the movement started to surface publicly. Immense pressure was thrust on the political leadership of Hamas when, upon unexpectedly winning the elections, it found itself faced almost overnight with hitherto unexperienced challenges. Hamas's government came under immediate international siege, led by the United States and the European Union and involving even the United Nations, not to mention Israel, and this required creative and fast political initiatives. The luxury and time available for formulating every single political step to appease every faction of the internal membership, and for presenting those policies in an appealing format to the outside world as well, have come to an end. It is safe to say that the longer Hamas remains in power, the more tensions will appear between its religious and nationalist constituents, with the probable pragmatic outcome of pushing the movement to a more politicized nationalist leaning.

3 Hamas, Israel and Judaism

HAMAS'S VIEW OF THE JEWS

Is Hamas an anti-Semitic movement?

To start with, the term 'anti-Semitic' is highly problematic when it is used to describe Palestinian or Arab perceptions of Jews and Judaism, because Palestinians and Arabs are Semites themselves. Since it is indeed self-contradictory within an Arab context, a more accurate term to describe certain Palestinian and/or Arab attitudes towards Jews might be 'anti-Jewish'.

In their historic context, the indigenous Muslims, Christians and Jews of the Middle East lived together with a remarkable degree of coexistence, particularly when compared with the lack of religious tolerance and the predominance of religious fanaticism in medieval Christian Europe. Jews in particular enjoyed a 'golden era' of centuries-long peaceful living under Islamic rule, in what is known now as the Middle East and North Africa, and particularly in Andalusia. Tolerance toward Jews and Christians in Islamic tradition and societies is underpinned by the *Quran*, where the common roots of Islam, Judaism and Christianity in the Old Testament are acknowledged, and respect for Jews and Christians by Muslims is required. Thus, in principle there is no theological basis for religious (as well as ethnic or racial) discrimination that could lead to European-type anti-Semitism and its manifestations.

Ironically, the strong anti-Jewish feelings that crept into the

Middle East by the start of the twentieth century originated in Europe, from European ideas compounded by European actions. Since the early twentieth century, European Zionism exploited the ever-growing European desire to resolve the 'Jewish question' (a question astoundingly and notoriously exacerbated by the events of World War II in Nazi-occupied Europe), ultimately by exporting the Jewish populations outside Europe and marrying the solution with the Jewish aspiration of creating a Jewish state in Palestine. With the establishment of Israel by dictat and at the expense of the indigenous Palestinians who had peaceably occupied their lands for over two thousand years, Jews and Zionists, and Judaism and Zionism, became conjoined. With half of the Palestinian people forced out of their homes and lands on the eve of the formation of Israel in 1948, the western-exported Jewry forcibly replaced them, all under the approving eye of Europe and the United States. Thus, the Jews/Zionists came to be seen in the eyes of Palestinians and Arabs as a form of colonial military occupation, consequently destroying the peaceful coexistence of Muslims and Jews that had prevailed in the region for centuries.

The spurious 'anti-Semitic' book *The Protocols of the Elders of Zion* (which also originated in Europe) described the Jews as masterminding a global conspiracy to control the world. It suddenly found a ripe climate in Palestine because of the creation of Israel in the Palestinian homelands in 1948. This date ended the peaceful period of coexistence between Muslims and Jews, and unfolded a new chapter of bloody relationships and hatred.

Unless this background is taken into account, any understanding of the explicit or implicit attitudes in Hamas to Jews is unlikely. Intrinsically and religiously Hamas could not be anti-Jewish. By virtue of Islamic religious teachings, Hamas, or any other Islamic individual or group, is prohibited from inflicting any harm on Jews simply because they are Jews (or Christians, or any other group for that matter). So to be factually correct,

Hamas is strongly anti-Zionist, not anti-Jew, with the term Zionist defined as 'a person or group whose focus is the establishment of a Jewish state in Palestine'. (The name comes from Zion, the hill upon which the oldest part of Jerusalem was built.) Although in the early years of its inception Hamas made little effort to differentiate between Judaism as a religion and Zionism as a political movement, in later and recent years Hamas has completely clarified its thinking on this issue. It is anti-Zionist, not anti-Jew.

But surely Hamas's Charter is full of 'anti-Jewish' statements?

It is true that many 'anti-Jewish' statements do exist in the Hamas Charter of 1988. Not only is it also true that eight years later these statements are irrelevant to the present Hamas party, the Charter itself has become largely obsolete. The Charter was written in early 1988 by one individual and was made public without appropriate general Hamas consultation, revision or consensus, to the regret of Hamas's leaders in later years. The author of the Charter was one of the 'old guard' of the Muslim Brotherhood in the Gaza Strip, completely cut off from the outside world. All kinds of confusions and conflations between Judaism and Zionism found their way into the Charter, to the disservice of Hamas ever since, as this document has managed to brand it with charges of 'anti-Semitism' and a naïve worldview.

Hamas leaders and spokespeople have never referred to the Charter or quoted from it, evidence that it has come to be seen as a burden rather than an intellectual platform that embraces the movement's principles. The sophisticated language of the Hamas discourse on the eve of its assuming power after the 2006 elections, and the language and discourse of the Charter of 1988, almost appear to describe two completely different movements.

Indeed, just two years after the publication of the 1988

Charter loaded with anti-Jewish rhetoric, Hamas published documents in 1990 distancing itself from what had been included in the Charter. Emphasizing that its struggle has been merely against Zionists and Zionism, not against the Jews and Judaism, it drew a clear distinction between the two:

> The non-Zionist Jew is one who belongs to the Jewish culture, whether as a believer in the Jewish faith or simply by accident of birth, but ... [who] takes no part in aggressive actions against our land and our nation .... Hamas will not adopt a hostile position in practice against anyone because of his ideas or his creed but will adopt such a position if those ideas and creed are translated into hostile or damaging actions against our people.

Discussing this differentiation with the author, one of Hamas's leaders went so far as to say that 'being Jewish, Zionist or Israeli is irrelevant, what is relevant for me is the notion of occupation and aggression. Even if this occupation was imposed by an Arab or Islamic state and the soldiers were Arabs or Muslims I would resist and fight back.'

On the ground however, in Palestinian cities and refugee camps in the West Bank and the Gaza Strip, ordinary people, including Hamas members, do use the terms 'Jew', 'Zionist' and 'Israeli' interchangeably. On the surface, mixing up these terms blurs the differences: clearly not every Jew is a Zionist, and not every Israeli is a Zionist. However regrettably imprecise the use of any of these terms interchangeably might be in common parlance, it is somewhat irrelevant in the face of the ongoing presence of an aggressive, illegal and non-Palestinian occupier, which whatever distinctions are made is identifiably Jewish (Zionist/Israeli). It is the aggression and occupation that is most relevant, whichever way it gets labelled in the heat of day-to-day confrontation.

Though this should be borne in mind, a type of undeniable anti-Jewishness has come to cut across Palestinian and Arab societies. It is not based on religious, racial or cultural hatred, as in the western rubric 'anti-Semitism'. The roots of any anti-Jewishness in Arab society are entirely political, in response to aggression, and any other form of anti-Jewishness would be completely refuted from the perspective of Islamic theology. Military actions taken against 'Jewish' targets are taken against them as representatives of an illegal, aggressive occupier, and have nothing whatsoever to do with their creed, race or non-Islamic culture.

In Hamas's view, what would be the future of the Jews in Palestine?

Hamas's views on this question are rather vague. In Hamas's early years a standard answer would have been that the Palestinian Jews whose forebears had lived on the land in peace and coexistence with its Muslim inhabitants for centuries would be welcome to stay on in a future Palestinian state. They are, after all, first and foremost Palestinians. Western and other foreign Jews, on the other hand, who had migrated to Palestine from all parts of the world, should return to their countries of origin. In fact this view was commonly shared by Palestinians and Arabs for a long time after the establishment of the state of Israel in 1948, before it gradually faded away. This view has long since been realized to be unrealistic, and has almost completely dropped out of Hamas's discourse. But Hamas has formulated no new answer to fill in the void.

The dilemma that Hamas – and the Palestinian intelligentsia at large – have faced concerning this issue is that generations of young Jews with western and worldwide ancestry have been born on historically Palestinian soil as the years of this conflict have dragged on. Of course this is an issue that is part and parcel of the larger 'demographic dimension' to the conflict, which worries both the Palestinians and the Israelis.

Population projections suggest that in the very near future there will be roughly equal numbers of Jews and Palestinians living in the historic land of Palestine. The spectre of demography, and in particular who will overrule whom in the not so distant future, concerns both parties. Israeli solutions have revolved around annexing the maximum amount of Palestinian land with the minimum Palestinian population on it, to preserve the Jewishness of the state in the long run. Palestinian solutions have been to fight to stay on their lands (in the West Bank and the Gaza Strip), defying direct and indirect Israeli measures to force as many of them as possible to leave, and upholding the right to return for refugees whom the Israelis have managed to expel.

Hamas has attempted to break away from the limited thinking that can only imagine Palestinians and Israelis squeezed into 'Palestine/Israel'. A reluctant idea that appears now and then in Hamas's discourse is that Palestine in the future should be part of a wider union of Arab and Muslim territories. In this case, even if the Jews were the majority within the confines of whatever part of historic Palestine they might ultimately claim, they would lose any numerical superority when the remaining territory of Palestine was merged with other Arab territories. The overwhelming Arab majority in the neighbouring countries, who would mix with the population in Palestine, would serve to neutralize the effects of any Jewish majority in Palestine.

A rather less far-fetched view that is, again reluctantly, talked about by Hamas is the one-state solution, based on equality and citizenship, but only if the (more or less five million) Palestinian refugees were given the right to return to their cities and villages in Israel. Israel takes no notice of this idea, saying that it would implicitly carry with it the death of the state of Israel by eroding once and for all its Jewish nature and majority.

Hamas, it seems, will have to grapple for a while longer with the question of the future of the Jews in Palestine.

HAMAS'S VIEW OF ISRAEL

What is Israel in Hamas's eyes?

According to Hamas, Israel is a colonial state established by force and resulting from western colonialism and imperialism against Arabs and Muslims before and after the turn of the twentieth century. To the left and right of this central view, there are other perceptions that feed into each other, and sometimes coincide with perceptions held by more secular Palestinian groups. In the early years of its formation Hamas's view of Israel was loaded with religious significance, holding that Israel was the culmination of a Jewish onslaught against Muslims and their holy places in Jerusalem. The establishment of Israel with the strong support of Western powers was seen as a renewal of the medieval Crusades.

The discourse of Hamas has, however, become more developed and adaptive to modern realities. Its views on Israel, accordingly, have been recast within the parameters of occupation/occupier, with the main drive of resistance against Israel directed against its aggression, not its religion. It would be inaccurate to suggest that this development in the discourse of Hamas has sprung from deep roots, or that is has completely replaced the old language, laden with religious antagonism to Israel. But in general parlance the political discourse that is delivered by the Hamas leadership and included in its official statements and documents on Israel is now based mostly on the language of international law, and on political, not religious, assumptions.

Is Hamas planning the destruction of Israel?

The phrase 'the destruction of Israel', as often used by the media when referring to Hamas's 'ultimate goal', is in fact never used or adopted by Hamas, even in its most radical statements. Hamas's ultimate slogan is 'the liberation of Palestine', which falls short of saying what would actually be done with Israel should that goal be achieved. In its rather obsolete Charter issued in early 1988 (see Chapter 9), which is crammed with rhetoric that is embarrassing to the Hamas of today, there are statements that could be interpreted as referring to the destruction of Israel. However, the entire document is of minimal present value, and hardly corresponds to any realities and thinking that Hamas lives and expresses currently.

Realistically speaking, the argument that 'Hamas's tacit and ultimate end is the destruction of Israel' bears no relevance. The facts and positions on the ground speak for themselves, and tend completely in the opposite direction. Neither Hamas nor any other Palestinian or Arab party – or even state for that matter – has any dream of having the ability to destroy Israel. Israel enjoys military capabilities, both conventional and non-conventional, that would enable it to destroy all of its neighbouring countries in the Middle East in a matter of days. It is an uncontested fact that there is no threat to the existence of Israel in either the medium and long term, but there certainly is one against the Palestinians posed by Israel. Depicting Hamas (and the Palestinians) as any such threat to Israel is a matter of political propaganda and emotional sensationalism.

In recent years Hamas has grown out of its early naive discourse of the late 1980s, and today's Hamas projects are more nuanced and its pronouncements more realistic. The dominant theme of its political and military discourse is resistance against the occupation of illegally seized lands and driving the occupiers out of the West Bank and Gaza Strip. Since Hamas took control of the Palestinian Authority after elections in 2006 it has not expressed a single word of the old rhetoric of the Charter, or issued any ill-considered slogans.

In summary, any suggestion that Hamas plans or aims to destroy Israel is obviously naive. For Hamas to be able to achieve such a goal it would have to remain in power for decades, defeating all the Palestinian groups that would not work toward that goal. It would also have to build a massive Palestinian army in the West Bank and the Gaza Strip over decades, with Israel unconcernedly looking on. It would have to import tanks and jet fighters, from sympathetic international sources that do not exist, and train hundreds of thousands of soldiers on the tiny strips of non-contiguous land it would control. How could Hamas possibly defeat Israel militarily, let alone destroy it, when all other Arab countries collectively have failed to do so in the past half-century?

Despite what euphoria Hamas has seemed to enjoy at its high peaks, both militarily in its waves of successful suicide attacks in the heart of Israeli cities, and politically in its election victory in 2006, Hamas remains defensive rather than offensive. The structural confines that limit Palestinians in general apply to Hamas as well, and sometimes even more so because of the specificity of the movement (such as the lack of international support, as was the case with the PLO). Wary of its difficult position, Hamas's engagement in politics and world affairs is mostly driven by defensive mechanisms. Its ultimate goal in the coming years will be simply to preserve its own existence and avoid destruction, not to destroy others.

Would Hamas ever recognize Israel and conclude peace agreements with it?

It is not inconceivable that Hamas would recognize Israel. Hamas's pragmatism and its realistic approach to issues leave ample room for such a development. Yet most of the conditions that could create a conducive climate for such a step lie in the hands of the Israelis. As long as Israel refuses to acknowledge the basic rights of the Palestinian people in any end result based on the principle of a two-state solution, Hamas will find it impossible to recognize Israel.

Despite the often-cited rhetoric in Hamas's discourse about the impossibility of recognizing Israel, there actually is a visible thread of thinking that offers just such a possibility, though only if Israel reciprocated positively. After assuming his new post in early April 2006, Hamas's foreign minister Mahmoud al-Zahhar sent a letter to Kofi Annan, the Secretary-General of the United Nations, declaring that his government would be willing to live in peace, side by side with 'its neighbours', based on a two-state solution. However, other statements attributed to Hamas leaders have implied that the issue of recognizing Israel should be one of the goals of negotiations, not the prerequisite to them.

If Israel shows no interest in dealing with Hamas, and insists on 'unilateral measures' that perpetuate the occupational status quo, Hamas will never recognize Israel. If this were to be the only proffered political climate, the maximum that the movement could accept would be a long-term truce, and it would avoid and evade recognizing Israel to the end.

That a peace treaty could be concluded between Israel and Hamas, however, is not implausible. Hamas enjoys influence, legitimacy and a clean record in governance among the Palestinians, furnishing it with the political capital needed to negotiate with Israel. Attempting to find some leeway between its past declarations about non-recognition of Israel and the pressing realities at hand, the movement has created a distinction between the government of Hamas and Hamas as an organization. Implicitly, this means that Hamas's government is ready to go beyond the standard and well-known declarations of Hamas as a party. Yet again, the extent to which Hamas could go down the course of negotiating with Israel is strongly contingent on the positions offered by the latter.

To reconcile the extreme of the liberation of the entire historic land of Palestine (which is unlikely to be achieved) with the realities of the existence of Israel on the ground, Hamas has suggested resorting to a national referendum on the final settlement to be concluded by Israel and the Palestinians. The democratically elected Hamas will abide by whatever the Palestinian people decide concerning their own fate, in a free and democratic referendum. By Hamas's way of thinking, the referendum idea is a decent solution to the theoretical and practical impasse that could result, and be exclusively, if wrongly, put down to Hamas's refusal to recognize Israel and accept the principle of a two-state solution. If peace talks led to the drafting of a peace treaty that required the 'negotiating parties' to recognize each other (and it was a treaty in which Palestinian rights were acknowledged and granted in a manner likely to be satisfactory to the Palestinians), then Hamas would accept any decision taken by the people on such a treaty via the mechanism of a referendum. Hamas as an organization says publicly that under such conditions it would have no choice but to respect the will and decision endorsed by the Palestinian people.

4 Hamas's resistance and military strategy

FORCING UNCONDITIONAL ISRAELI WITHDRAWAL

What is Hamas's 'program(me) of resistance'?

'Resistance' as a concept is the most central principle in the thinking and formation of Hamas; it is even part of its very name, 'the Islamic Resistance Movement'. When Hamas was established in late 1987, the Palestinian and Arab political climate was still absorbing the shock created by Egypt's recognition of Israel and the peace treaty concluded by both countries in 1982. Negotiation, rather than armed struggle, was being put forward emphatically as a means to achieve political goals, including the restoration of occupied land. In the same year of 1982, the PLO was defeated by Israel in Lebanon and consequently all Palestinian guerrillas and their leadership were forced to leave the country and move to Tunis. The logic of using armed resistance to liberate Palestine had thus suffered two major blows in one year. Since then, and with the new North African PLO base very far from Palestine, a strategy of peace negotiations and initiatives started to dominate over the armed struggle approach. The PLO itself became far more lenient than before on the issue of negotiation with Israel and the principle of a two-state solution.

By contrast, in reiterating and reaffirming the concept of 'resistance' Hamas was declaring its position against any negotiated settlement with Israel, and injecting new blood in a somewhat fading concept. The only way to regain Palestinian rights, Hamas vehemently suggested with rising confidence, was through resistance against the colonial occupation and wresting back rights from the enemy. Hamas's logic came down to the idea that wherever a military occupation exists, a military resistance should be expected. Such resistance, in all its various forms, would only stop when the occupation ended.

All Hamas's conduct, policies and actions emanate from and are justified by this conviction. However, there have been few specific details offered about how matters would proceed beyond this concept, particularly on how the 'withdrawal' of the occupying troops would take place, or what would follow it. Hamas's leaders have kept repeating, 'Withdraw first, and then we take things as they come.'

This 'strategy' of Hamas, which in effect spells out no long-term strategy, might appear on the surface to be futile and shallow. Yet, at a more fundamental level, it has proved successful and pragmatic for the organization. First, its plain terminology and uncompromising simplicity have been hard to argue against; second, this same single focus and simplicity conceals Hamas's theological arguments, which are more difficult to sell; third, it provides an uncomplicated theoretical umbrella under which Hamas's military and non-military actions of 'resistance' can easily be conducted.

Throughout Hamas's lifetime, beginning in late 1987, various forms of resistance have been deployed, ranging from popular uprisings, mobilization, strikes, and military attacks against the Israeli army and settlers, to executing suicide bombings in the heart of Israeli cities. These have been deployed either in combination or separately, but in all cases using whichever method has corresponded to the specific political environment prevailing at the time. The ultimate aim of any combination of all sorts of resistance, in Hamas's thinking, is to force unconditional Israeli withdrawal. The struggle of all Palestinian organizations, including of course the PLO and its factions, and the Palestinian Authority which was established in the West Bank and Gaza Strip in 1993/4, has been focused on achieving such a withdrawal. However, Hamas wants it without surrendering any other Palestinian rights in return, and without the recognition of Israel. The PLO and other Palestinian factions have come to terms with a reciprocal recognition with Israel based on the two-state solution. Hamas will not accept this, but might accept a formula that tacitly recognizes the *de facto* existence of Israel but without formally recognizing any right of Israel to exist. This is because regardless of whether the withdrawal resulted directly from peace talks or by force, Hamas could logically insist that it take place without compromising any additional Palestinian rights, or issues such as sovereignty over East Jerusalem, the position of borders and the right of Palestinian refugees to return.

How has Hamas's 'programme of resistance' materialized on the ground?

Hamas believes that the unilateral Israeli withdrawal from the Gaza Strip in 2005 validates its strategy of resistance. Various declarations by Hamas representatives have stated that the withdrawal was the result, to a large part if not fully, of the continuous resistance and long-term pressure on the Israeli troops and settlers in the Strip, which left Israel with no option but to yield and withdraw. Many other Palestinians, however, refute this view and call into suspicion Israel's real purpose and intention in taking this step. They fear that Israel has withdrawn from the Gaza Strip, which has no strategic or religious value to the Jewish state, in order to concentrate and consolidate its occupation and control over the West Bank and Jerusalem, where the true battle between the Palestinians and the Israelis lies.

In the West Bank, too, Hamas believes that carrying out

cycles of confrontation against the occupation will make the
cost of the Israeli presence there unsustainable; that multiplying
Israeli costs in terms of human loss, draining of resources,
mounting internal tension and deteriorating image worldwide
will eventually bear fruit. When upon winning the Israeli elections in March 2006 the Kadima party made public its intention
to undertake unilateral partial withdrawals from certain areas in
the West Bank, Hamas claimed part of the credit. It argued,
again, that had there been no resistance with costly consequences to Israel, any withdrawal, however small, would have
only been undertaken in return for excessive Palestinian
concessions.

It is worth mentioning that Hamas points to the experience of
Hizbullah, which was perceived to have forced Israel to withdraw
unconditionally from south Lebanon in 2000. At that time the
Israeli step was taken for a variety of reasons, including the
diminishing chances of the Israeli occupation in that area achieving any strategic objectives, and the mounting questioning of the
value of that occupation by Israeli decision makers and the Israeli
public as well. That of course was in addition to the continuous,
conspicuous and highly emotive daily losses, notably on the side
of Israeli soldiers. Hizbullah naturally chose to focus on this last
factor exclusively, to vindicate its 'resistance strategy'. Likewise,
Hamas has underlined the same factor, calling Palestinians to
emulate Hizbullah in exerting extreme pressure on the Israeli
occupation to force unilateral withdrawal.

What is the intifada *(as in the first* intifada *of 1987 and the
second* intifada *of 2000)?*

Intifada is the Arabic word for a popular uprising. Within the
Palestinian context it evokes sentimental connotations, since
popular uprisings, or *intifadas*, typically and historically marked
certain turning points in the course of the Palestinian national
struggle in the past decades. During the British mandate over

Palestine (1922–48), Palestinian uprisings were directed against the British, with the most significant one occurring in 1936.

In the era of the Israeli occupation *intifadas* were almost the only effective means at the disposal of the Palestinians. Apart from small-scale uprisings and forms of resistance, the two major *intifadas* erupted in 1987 and 2000. The 1987 uprising took place initially in the Gaza Strip on 8 December, then the spark moved to the cities of the West Bank. The causes that led to the *intifada* were multifold and fed off each other. They were the escalation of brutality by the Israeli occupation, and the growing anger among Palestinians in response to the humiliation of the occupation – not only politically, but in the very real way that the occupation had reduced those areas to soul-destroying poverty – and the rising power of the Islamists, who were compelled to adopt a new confrontational policy against Israel, as has been discussed earlier in the book.

The immediate causes that actually ignited the *intifada* were a series of events linked to the escape of a number of Palestinian prisoners who hid in one of the refugee camps, then killed an Israeli settler. In response to the killing, an Israeli truck ran down some Palestinian workers, killing four and wounding nine others. Consequently, angry Palestinians took to the streets of the Gaza Strip in the following days in unprecedented mass demonstrations. If the early days of the *intifada* were spontaneous with no organizational planning behind them, the following days witnessed heavy engagement and even rivalry between the Palestinian organizations, including the newly established Hamas, to spearhead the *intifada* and keep it going.

The 1987 *intifada* was mostly a weaponless confrontation, relying instead on mobilizing people, mass demonstrations and throwing stones at Israeli soldiers. Hence it was called the 'stones revolution'. It did not witness the practice of suicide bombing, which was a couple more years in coming. Erratically waxing and waning, the *intifada* lasted roughly until 1993 when the Oslo Accords were signed between Israel and the PLO, resulting for the first time in a Palestinian form of authority in the West Bank and the Gaza Strip.

The second *intifada* took place in September 2000. The causes behind this *intifada* were somewhat different. After seven years of the Oslo Accords with Israel, which had promised the Palestinians a sovereign and independent state by the end of the year 1999, the Palestinian public lost confidence in the process and became frustrated. Through those Accords it had been hoped that an interim period of five years, starting in 1993, would end in resolving the major issues of the conflict including Jerusalem, the control of borders, dismantling the Israeli settlements in the West Bank and the Gaza Strip, and the status of refugees.

Contrary to those hopes, all evidence pointed to the fact that the Israeli occupation was tightening its grip, and that the newly set-up Palestinian Authority was being restricted in effect to administrating much of the occupation – from the prosaic daily services of the population, to actually maintaining the security of Israel and its settlers from Palestinian attacks. The size and population of Israeli settlements on land that was supposed to have been returned to the Palestinians almost doubled during the years following the Oslo Agreement. The status of Jerusalem, a major issue of the conflict yet to be resolved in negotiation, was swept under heavier Israeli control. By the eve of the second *intifada*, the peace process brought about by the Oslo Accords was witnessing the first signs of its own demise.

The immediate spark of the 2000 intifada was Ariel Sharon's provocative visit to al-Harm al-Shirif, the holiest Muslim site in Jerusalem, which infuriated Palestinians. Against much advice Sharon, then the leader of the Likud opposition party, decided to make a point for political purposes against the ruling Israeli Labour party, that even the holiest of Muslim places in Jerusalem were under full Israeli control and jurisdiction.

Although it started as a popular uprising with no use of weapons, the second *intifada* quickly turned into an armed confrontation. Palestinians across the political spectrum supported the *intifada*: the ruling PA organizations, such as Fatah and other PLO factions, stood side by side with Hamas and other opposition factions.

Will Hamas disarm itself voluntarily or be disarmed at all forcibly if needed?

'What you get from anyone, or on a negotiating table should match your strength on the ground', Sheikh Ahmad Yasin, the founder of Hamas, was once quoted as saying. 'Strength' is interpreted in all forms, with the military figures on the top. Thus, since its inception in late 1987, Hamas (and other Palestinian factions) have amassed considerable caches of weapons mainly in the Gaza Strip but also in the West Bank. These include machine guns, bombs, and homemade rockets with a range of a few kilometres and capable of striking Israeli settlements if launched from parts of the Gaza Strip.

In terms of quality, quantity and military effectiveness, Hamas's weapons, and all other Palestinian weapons combined for that matter, have never amounted to a serious threat to the state of Israel. These weapons could only inflict harm in the form of guerrilla attacks, quick and short shootouts and suicide bombings. Sources for acquiring weaponry include smuggling it in from Egypt (against the policy of the Egyptian government of course), and buying Israeli weapons from 'black markets' and from discontented individuals in the Palestinian security forces who were armed officially by the Palestinian Authority. Hamas has also developed local manufacture of primitive weapons, notably bombs and short-range rockets, based on domestic material.

During and after the second *intifada* of 2000, it was obvious that Hamas's military power had reached new peaks, particularly in the Gaza Strip, paralleling that of the Palestinian Authority. On the eve of its landslide victory in the January 2006 elections in the West Bank and the Gaza Strip, it was believed that Hamas's arsenal of weapons could furnish the movement with the enormous leverage that goes hand in hand with its political and popular influence.

There is considerable consensus among observers that Hamas's weaponry, used and supervised by its military wing Izzedin al-Qassam, is under the tight control of the movement. Apart from a few factional incidents where Hamas members used weapons, their use is strictly limited to the struggle with Israel. Also, this weaponry has clearly provided Hamas with a deterrent against other Palestinian rivals, mainly the Fatah movement and the Palestinian Authority.

The situation in the Gaza Strip has been marked by chaos and a multiplicity of centres of power since the eruption of the first *intifada* in 1987. Accessibility to arms has created a hard-to-control environment, and factional rivalry has brought Palestinians to the verge of civil war on more than one occasion. When the Palestinian Authority was established in 1993/4 one of its main responsibilities, pressed on it by Israel under the Oslo Accords, was to control the chaotic situation and unify the 'Palestinian arms' under its control. Stridently Hamas refused any proposal to hand in its weapons to the Palestinian Authority, or any suggestion in the direction of giving the Palestinian Authority the slightest supervision over its weapons.

Ironically, when Hamas came to power after winning the elections of January 2006 and itself became the Palestinian Authority, it called upon other factions to unite their armed wings under one unified control under the supervision of Hamas in its new PA role. As was to be expected, Fatah's military wing and other factions refused Hamas's call.

In the short and medium terms, it is neither likely that Hamas would disarm voluntarily, nor conceivable that it could be disarmed forcibly by other parties (including Israel and other Palestinian groups). Hamas keeps repeating its position that its arms are there to defend the Palestinian people and their rights, and insofar as Israeli continues to occupy Palestinian land, and those rights are not realized, armed struggle and all it entails should stay at the heart of Hamas, and thus at the moment, of official Palestinian strategy.

SUICIDE ATTACKS

When and why has Hamas adopted suicide bombing as a strategy?

Hamas's suicide attacks against Israeli civilians are justified by public statements made by its officials now and then, stating that these attacks are reciprocal actions. They are generated, Hamas says, in response to the Israeli killing of Palestinian civilians, and will end immediately once Israel declares that it will stop doing the same to Palestinians. Offers of negotiation by Hamas were made to civilians from both sides of the targeted killing, but met with categorical refusal from Israel on the grounds that it would 'do no business with terrorists'.

Although Hamas came into being in 1987, its trademark suicide attacks did not begin until 1994. The first wave of these attacks was carried out in retaliation for the Hebron massacre, in which a fanatic Israeli settler killed 29 Palestinian worshippers in the Abraham Mosque in February 1994. Hamas vowed to take revenge and it did so by blowing up Israeli soldiers, settlers and civilians in the hearts of Israeli cities. At that point Hamas discovered the spectacular effect this kind of attack had on the public imagination, and embraced it. Realizing that targeting civilians deliberately can be a dangerous strategy, Hamas has been careful to link any suicide bombing that it has undertaken to specific Israeli killings of Palestinian civilians.

Prior to 1994 Hamas's policies were clear in attacking only 'legitimate military targets'. The major shift to targeting civilians, even with the justification of only retaliating for a civilian killing with another civilian killing, has nonetheless incurred heavy costs to Hamas. Defying Israel's violent retaliation against Hamas, epitomized by the Israeli strategy of assassinating its leaders, the movement has geared up its use of suicide operations over the years. It had realized that although these operations rallied the international community against Hamas, and distorted somewhat the image of the legitimate Palestinian struggle, they provided the movement with an aura of strength and popularity amongst the Palestinian people themselves. The Palestinians started to look at Hamas as an organization capable of inflicting damage on the Israelis and taking revenge for any Israeli killing of Palestinians.

Lacking any effective means to defend its civilians against these suicide attacks, Israel was devastated by them. The horror of a potential bombing that could take place in any bus, shopping centre or restaurant brought Israeli cities at certain periods of time nearly to a complete state of terrifying suspense. Israel not only mobilized its military might to stamp out Hamas's infrastructure in the Gaza Strip and the West Bank, but also brought to bear all sorts of pressure, including external pressure. On more than one occasion Israel hinted, via unofficial mediators, that it was ready to talk to Hamas with a view to stopping these attacks. However Hamas adhered to its declared position: 'Stop killing Palestinian civilians and we will stop killing Israeli civilians.' Israel repeatedly refused this offer.

Sheikh Yasin succinctly articulated Hamas's policy on suicide bombings in September 2003. When asked whether the attacks would continue irrespective of circumstances, he replied in the negative, and explained, 'If we perceive that the atmosphere favors such a decision, we stop. And when we perceive that the atmosphere has changed, we carry on.' In general, the wider the gap between the peace strategy and the attainment of Palestinian rights, the more room Hamas has to pursue its resistance strategy.

Politically and strategically, Hamas became aware that, at certain junctures, using suicide attacks had become its strongest card in the conflict with Israel, as well as with its rivalry with the Palestinian Authority and its Fatah movement. Relinquishing this card would only be considered if there was really a possibility of a worthy return. Continuous Israeli military efforts, coupled with repetitive crackdowns on Hamas by the security forces of the Palestinian Authority, failed to destroy Hamas's capability in undertaking these attacks. Political and diplomatic pressures were also exerted on Hamas by Egypt, Jordan and the European Union in order to compel the movement to stop these attacks, at least temporarily. In finding itself on the receiving end of much high condemnation for the suicide bombings both regionally and internationally, Hamas discovered that the exact same attention regionally and internationally was also furnishing them with further leverage.

On several occasions Hamas has shown flexibility in temporarily halting its attacks, either to avoid straying from a collective agreement among Palestinian factions, or to prove its pragmatism. In late 1995 it stopped suicide attacks for months, only to resume them after the Israeli assassination of one of its military leaders, Yahya Ayyash. Similar halt–resume 'tacit agreements' took place during the second *intifada* (2000–05) for short periods of time, but all failed because Israel would waste no opportunity to assassinate one Hamas leader after another.

How many Israelis has Hamas killed? And how many Hamas members have the Israelis killed or imprisoned, and what have been the most noteworthy attacks committed by Hamas?

Hamas's suicide attacks have given the movement a bad name by enabling Israel to succeed in selling an image of Hamas as a mere 'terrorist organisation' whose sole purpose is the killing of innocent Israeli civilians. The justness of the Palestinian cause has paid a high price because of them, as Israel has exploited the attacks by reducing the nature of the Palestinian struggle to an issue of 'terrorism and counter-terrorism'. The worldwide condemnation of the Palestinian killing of Israelis is gravely uneven compared with the mild condemnation of similar Israeli killings of Palestinians. The number of Israelis killed by Hamas (and all other Palestinian factions combined) from Hamas's

inception in December 1987 until April 2006 amounted to only a
quarter of the number of the Palestinians killed by Israel over the
same period of time.

The killing of civilians on both sides is inhumane, and to deal
with dead civilians as mere statistics implies a measure of insen-
sitivity. Yet the statistics help to further the understanding of the
whole picture. The aggregate figures of the statistics provided by
the Israeli human rights organisation Btselem (www.btselem.org)
show that 1,426 Israelis, military personnel and civilians, were
killed by Palestinian factions, compared with 5,050 Palestinians
killed by Israel during those years. Of those casualties, there were
137 Israeli children (or under 18) killed against 998 Palestinian
children of the same age group.

What is the truce (hudna) *that Hamas offers?*

Hamas's defiance of both continuous Israeli attacks and mounting
international criticism against its suicide operations has been
accompanied by the offer of a *hudna* – the religious Islamic
concept of the classical notion of a truce, though with certain
differences – with the aim of easing pressure. The *hudna* is a rather
flexible traditional Islamic war practice which was first used by the
Prophet Muhammad in the famous Hodaibiya *hudna,* when in 628
AD he concluded with his enemies a ten-year truce, during which
people of the two parties were to live in peace. Later in Islamic
history *hudna* were used by different rulers to achieve different
goals, hence the flexibility and broad meaning of the concept. The
debate remains open among Muslim scholars whether the *hudna*
concept is merely a tactical ceasefire or a more sophisticated
practice which lays the groundwork for non-violent solutions.

Bound by its religious roots, Hamas has felt the need to
justify its adoption of any controversial policy on Islamic religious grounds. Hamas's offer of a truce would seem to contradict
its leading principle of *Jihad* – military struggle – against Israel.
Similarly, refraining from military struggle was the approach that

was officially adopted by the PLO and the Palestinian Authority and which ended in peace negotiations with Israel which were, in turn, strongly opposed by Hamas. To yield to a ceasefire Hamas would be seen to be simply following in the footsteps of its rivals, risking the loss of its distinctiveness.

Thus, by offering the *hudna* Hamas has been very keen to distinguish this concept from the practice of the PLO and the Palestinian Authority, which has always been described by Hamas as capitulation. There are two main distinctions that Hamas draws between a ceasefire and a *hudna*. The first is that a *hudna* is only an agreement on halting hostilities, not a peace treaty which could comprise concessions, and the second is that a ceasefire has lately come to imply an open-ended agreement whereas the *hudna* is limited by a period of time that is agreed between the belligerent parties. If the PLO and the Palestinian Authority are ready to abandon armed struggle and promote a lasting ceasefire, Hamas is not ready to do the same. The furthest that it could do, the *hudna* argument runs, is to agree on ten or 20 years of ceasefire without compromising on Palestinian rights. The *hudna* would calm down the situation, end violence and save the blood of civilians. The question, of course, is what would happen after the *hudna*? Hamas's answer is that the next step would depend on the acceptable behaviour of Israel and its intentions: the *hudna* could be renewed or ended.

On several separate occasions, Hamas has offered a *hudna* to Israel. The late Sheikh Ahmad Yasin was the first to suggest the idea back in 1993. Since then Hamas figures have repeated the offer, sometimes changing the period of time that it included (ten, 20 or even 30 years). Israel has always ridiculed the offer, yet some Israeli politicians conceive it to represent a pragmatic element in Hamas that should be encouraged. When Hamas came to power and controlled the Palestinian Authority in January 2006, it renewed its offer of a *hudna* to Israel for from 10 to 20 years.

5 Hamas's political and social strategy

HAMAS'S POSITION ON THE VARIOUS PEACE PLANS WITH ISRAEL

Why does Hamas reject the peace agreements reached by the PLO and Israel in 1993/4, known as the Oslo Accords?

The original Palestinian position concerning the creation of Israel in 1948 was a complete Palestinian consensus to reject any proposal that would situate Israel on any part of the historic land of Palestine. This position remained almost unchanged until 1988, when the Palestine Liberation Organization (PLO) publicly declared its readiness to accept the concept of a two-state solution: Palestine in the West Bank and Gaza Strip (less than a third of historic Palestine) and Israel in the rest of the land. By then Israel would not even entertain the proposal, and none of the major Israeli parties accepted that concept until very late in 2006 when the two-state solution was adopted by Ariel Sharon's Kadima party.

The balance of power has constantly favoured Israel, which has always enjoyed unreserved support from the United States and the West. Israel was thus under no pressure to even acknowledge the resolutions issued by the United Nations supporting the two-state solution and calling on Israel to withdraw from the territories it has occupied since the 1967 war. The Oslo Agreements in 1993/4 offered the Palestinians limited self-rule but only over the

Palestinian population – with no jurisdiction over Palestinian land – for five years, as a testing period. Should the Palestinians show 'good behaviour' then negotiations would be initiated to settle the major issues of the conflict, such as the fate or division of Jerusalem (which both 'states' claim as their rightful capital), the status of refugees, the dismantling of illegal Jewish settlements, control of borders and full sovereignty. From the Palestinian view-point, throughout the 'test period' the situation surrounding all the major contested issues has been exacerbated deliberately by Israel so that the resulting confrontational disorder would fail to meet the minimal requirements for any restitution of Palestinian rights. From the Israeli perspective, the Palestinians have clearly failed to prove that they are fit to be a 'partner' in peace, and thus no advancement should be undertaken to jointly solve the conflict.

Hamas's view has been that the Oslo Agreements, and any peace talks for that matter, are worthless as long as their design is built around a balance of power where the fulfilment of Israeli demands tops the agenda. According to Hamas, these are capitulation treaties, not peace agreements. From Hamas's perspective, the failure of the Oslo Accords is inevitable and the rationale behind this goes as follows:

> Oslo proponents claimed for months following its signing that it would bring an end to occupation [of Palestine] and that, therefore, the Palestinians need no longer exercise an armed struggle against the Israelis. But eight years after Oslo, the following have been the dividends of peace:
> 1. The territories occupied in 1967 are still occupied.
> 2. More than ever, the West Bank and Gaza have been carved up, mutilated and turned into isolated islands of human concentrations, or cantons, administered on behalf of the Israelis by the Palestinian Authority.
> 3. Existing illegal Jewish settlements continue to expand and new ones have been erected.

4. Jerusalem is being expanded and de-Arabised.
5. Large areas of land have been confiscated to allow for the construction of by-passes for the exclusive use of Jewish motorists and especially settlers who illegally live on confiscated Arab land.
6. Thousands of Palestinians continue to be detained in Israeli prisons.
7. Various forms of collective punishment continue to be adopted by the Israelis including the demolition of Palestinian homes, the closure of entire areas and the enforcement of economic blockades, the destruction of Palestinian infrastructure and the uprooting of trees and crops.
8. The economic situation for Palestinians is more dire than ever before.

In other words, the peace process has not improved by one iota the conditions of Palestinians under occupation and does not seem to promise any better future. The claim that armed struggle was no longer necessary (it should be noted here that no one within the Palestinian camp ever agreed that resistance was illegal) has been refuted by reality, giving credence to the Hamas argument (which is no different from the argument adopted before Oslo by the nationalist movement as a whole and that continues to be adopted by a score of Palestinian factions opposed to Oslo) that armed struggle is the only real means of liberation.

Hamas claims that by refusing ill-designed peace processes it upholds Palestinian rights and remains their defender. Hamas's opponents and critics in Palestinian circles and beyond say that the movement has not only offered no alternative, but was partly if not mostly responsible for the failure of the peace process when it continued its military attacks against Israel.

Popular referenda as a political programme

The political dilemma that Hamas has faced emanates from a realistic assumption: what is the reality if the majority of Palestinians accept a peace treaty with Israel that is still rejected by Hamas? If Hamas is adamant in staying true to its own principles, which consider peace treaties predominantly predicated on Israeli terms as akin to surrender, it is equally anxious to remain connected to and representative of the desires and aspirations of the majority of Palestinians. The solution to this dilemma was offered by Hamas through the idea of a referendum. This would mean that any form of final solution based on a negotiated settlement should be reached through a Palestinian consensus, which is achievable only by holding a referendum for all Palestinians inside and outside Palestine under international supervision.

In calling for a referendum Hamas wants more than to just rally the general Palestinian public into becoming strongly involved in deciding their own destiny. The movement is more concerned that at some point it will face the hard choice between continuing the armed struggle against the general mood of the Palestinian public, or becoming a purely political party. The referendum idea gives legitimacy to any future decision on the part of Hamas to abandon its armed activities. At the same time a collective popular vote on the final settlement would work to place the negotiating process and its results or compromises under bold popular scrutiny. This scrutiny, Hamas could then be assured, would surely be based on the preservation of Palestinian rights.

ELECTIONS, DEMOCRACY AND MOBILIZATION

Is Hamas genuinely democratic?

This is a standard rhetorical question which is always waved in the face of Islamist movements in the Middle East and elsewhere. There is little historic experience upon which one can judge accurately whether these movements have adopted democratic practices wholeheartedly. The same lack of actual history should also allow some benefit of the doubt. In the Middle Eastern context the question applies equally to all parties regardless of their political ideology. Democratic practice is visibly in short supply, and in the postcolonial era in the region there have been almost no fully fledged democracies. In Arab republics, nationalist and socialist parties have come to power, by either election or military coups, and have never relinquished power peacefully. In Arab monarchies, changing the system by democratic means has been out of the question. Thus, questioning how authentically democratic the Islamist movements are, in an environment that lacks democracy, implies considerable accusation as a starting point. In all the cases in the Middle East where ruling parties rejected democracy, or dismissed the results of elections because an opposition party won the majority, the intransigents were non-Islamist parties.

Therefore, Hamas is as genuine in its democratic conviction as any other political party, in a region inexperienced in this form of governance. There are, however, certain specificities in the make-up of Hamas that could help in exploring the level of its democratic credibility. Internally, the movement has embraced democratic practices in choosing its leaders. These practices have been well established and have even stretched less practicably to areas where democratic consensus might not have brought about ideal results. For example, when Hamas was in the process of forming its government in March 2006, the prime minister and all the cabinet ministers were elected by the rank and file. In the process, Hamas's cabinet ended up with a team of ministers that was not necessarily composed of the best people for their responsibilities. Instead of mandating the prime minister to form his government as a working unit based on professional and political considerations, all of the individual ministers were imposed on him in a democratic but perhaps more shambolic fashion from the party floor. It would appear that it could be safely said that there is no authoritarian system within Hamas as a party. In most cases, and at least in the Middle Eastern context, parties with authoritarian internal practices tend to import these qualities into their governments when they come to power.

It also must be remembered that Hamas has always defined itself as a resistance movement, essentially preoccupied with confronting the Israeli military occupation of Palestine. This occupation, with all its military resources, has always held the upper hand in this conflict, and controls every aspect of sovereignty over what has been left of any Palestinian state. All internal Palestinian politics take place under that control, and being voted in to take charge of a Palestinian government that functions under ultimate Israeli rule is hardly a great enticement to Hamas. Specifically because of the parameters of this foreign military control, Hamas never aspired to, or planned to, win a majority in any Palestinian elections, since this would have forced it into such an awkward position. Hamas's victory in the 2006 elections caught the movement by surprise, and it is hard to imagine Hamas wishing to cling to this awkward position by blocking or manipulating any coming elections. Given the 'siege' of protest and censure that it faces regionally and internationally, Hamas's biggest challenge will be to avoid total collapse and finish its four-year term in government with the least possible losses. Any scenario that has Hamas maneuvering to remain in such a compromised position of power by force is highly unlikely.

Within the Palestinian polity, especially in the post-Yasser Arafat era, the Palestinian political environment is not receptive to any kind of authoritarian rule. The centres of power have been fragmented and Hamas is at loggerheads with its rivals, particularly the Fatah movement. If Hamas decided to remain in power contrary to democratic practices, the immediate internecine result would be severe. Furthermore, the diversity of Palestinian society, the high level of education, and the general envy of the 'Israeli democracy' next door, narrow down any possibility of the development of an undemocratic Hamas. Secular, leftist and liberal lines of thought have been historically engraved all over

Palestinian society, no less upon the powerful Palestinian Christian community, which is highly politicized and active. Thus, even
if Hamas wanted to opt for any undemocratic form of politics the
surrounding internal circumstances would abort that option.

*What is the significance of Hamas's winning the Palestinian
elections of January 2006, and why did the Palestinians vote
for Hamas?*

Hamas's triumph in the 2006 elections was a complete shock for
all parties concerned, including Hamas itself. Hamas's plan was
to win a large enough number of seats, around 40 to 45 per cent,
to enable it to play the role of the guardian of the Palestinian
people's rights but without bearing the direct and ultimate responsibility of the government, which because of the Israeli control
was highly undesirable. The general thinking was by winning this
share of seats Hamas would easily form coalitions with other
smaller leftist opposition groups and would be capable of blocking any future compromises made by Fatah. The 'dirty' business
of day-to-day governing would still have been left to Fatah, but it
would have been hobbled politically in its negotiations with
Israel. The outcome of the elections, however, was a landslide
victory, with Hamas winning almost 60 per cent of the seats. The
defeat of Fatah was resounding.

The reasons behind the Hamas victory are multiple. In the
first place the movement harvested long years of devoted work
and popularity among Palestinians. At least half of the voters
supported Hamas outright for its programmes and declared objectives. The other half were driven by other forces. The failure of the
peace process combined with the ever-increasing Israeli brutality
had left Palestinians with no faith in negotiating a peaceful settlement with Israel. The balance in the debate surrounding peace
talks versus resistance was teetering, as the date for the elections
came nearer and nearer. The notion of 'peace talks' was clearly
losing ground, but there was no clear and definite support for the

'resistance' concept. The latter was vague, and many Palestinians were wary about its meaning and mechanisms. But the frustration of the peace talks took its toll and contributed largely to the defeat of the Fatah movement, the main force behind and upholder of the Oslo Accords and all that resulted from them.

Another major factor that helped Hamas in winning these elections was the failure in almost all areas of the Fatah-led Palestinian Authority. Not only did it fail externally in the peace talks with Israel, it also failed miserably internally, in managing the daily lives of the Palestinian people. Mismanagement, corruption and theft were the 'attributes' that came to be used to describe top leaders, ministers and their high-ranking staff. As unemployment and poverty reached unprecedented levels, the extravagant lifestyle of senior Palestinian officials infuriated the public, and it was the elections that empowered the people to punish those officials. Thus the elections proved to be the reaping season for both Hamas in its victory, and Fatah in its defeat.

It is easy to refute any suggestion that the Palestinian people voted for Hamas primarily on religious grounds. There was certainly no overnight popular conviction in favour of Hamas's religious or even political ideology. Christians and secular people voted for Hamas in various constituencies side by side with Hamas members and exponents. Hamas members also supported Christian candidates and won them seats in the parliament. Hamas itself appointed a Christian to its cabinet as the minister of tourism. The diverse nature of Hamas's voters confirmed that people were voting for Hamas as the nationalist liberation movement that promised change and reform on all fronts.

The victory itself is of paramount significance not only for Palestinians but also for Arabs, Muslims and beyond. At the Palestinian level it is a historic turning point, where a major shift in leadership has taken place. For the first time in more than half a century an Islamist group – grounded in national liberation – has moved into the driver's seat, replacing the secular leadership that had controlled Palestine's destiny and national decision-making process for decades. This fundamental change, furthermore, was realized through peaceful means and without violence, giving Hamas and all Palestinians a great sense of pride that they have embraced democracy and respect its outcome. It also gave them the chance to revisit the strategy over the conflict with Israel, which had been designed and pursued by the Fatah movement. For Hamas, this victory has represented the greatest challenge that the movement has faced since its inception. Almost overnight, all Hamas's ideals and slogans have been brought down to face realities on the ground. It could be safely said that the post-elections Hamas will be considerably different from the one before them.

At the Arab and Muslim level, Hamas's victory has been almost unique in that political Islam finally reached power, and in a democratic way. Islamist movements in the region were jubilant over Hamas's triumph and considered it as their own victory as well. Arab and Muslim regimes, on the other hand, have watched the rise of Hamas to power with worry and suspicion, fearing that its victory will encourage their local Islamists to pursue power more vigorously. Secular groups and individuals in the region have been divided. They support the nationalist liberation side of Hamas, but are anxious over its religious and social stance.

At the international level, a Palestinian government led by Hamas was regarded as a highly unpalatable fruit of democracy. The West in particular was caught in the dilemma of having to either accept such an undesirable result in order to show the Arab and Muslim world that its call for democracy in the region had been sincere, or be seen to cynically partake in an Israeli effort to bring down Hamas's government and risk losing any credibility.

HAMAS'S ECONOMIC OUTLOOK

What is Hamas's economic thinking?

Hamas has no distinct economic thinking or national programme that is any different from the 'free-market' basis that used to be the foundation of the Palestinian economy. This economy has been functioning for years, although it is weak and fragile by the standards of advanced capitalist states, because of crippling Israeli limitations and control. Unlike the Palestinian leftists, whose strong stamp of socialism colours their economic thinking, Hamas puts forth no particular economic ideology. Hamas as a party has never offered an integral vision of a so-called 'Islamic economy', which is sometimes referred to by individual Hamas figures.

By and large, the movement is content with the capitalist mode of economy which is based on free enterprise. It subscribes to the widespread belief within the circles of Islamist movements that Islam encourages free enterprise and enshrines the right to hold individual property. Therefore, the very basics of any 'Islamic economy' are close enough to the underlying tenets of capitalism. Yet the morality of such an 'Islamic economy' is closer to socialism. Many religious notions, such as a deep interest in justice and equality, obligatory systems of helping the poor, curbing monopolies and the prohibition of the unfair accumulation of fortunes, all echo the essences of socialist thought.

In practice, Hamas membership includes merchants, businesspeople and the rich. They have always been looked on with respect and admiration because of their continuous donations to the movement. Outside Palestine, rich Muslim businesspeople in the Gulf countries and other Muslim places represent the main source of Hamas's funding. Therefore, Hamas's experience of 'capitalism' and 'capitalist' people is somewhat positive. In recent years, however, there has been scattered criticism of the international economy and the monopolies of globalization, but these appear only in the margins of discussions of other major issues, such as the global hegemony of the United States.

In its attempt to secure a confidence vote from the Palestinian parliament in March 2006, the governing Hamas statement showed perhaps too much eagerness to emphasize its interest in encouraging foreign investors to come to Palestine and explore economic opportunities. Hamas vowed that:

> it would build the economic institutions of the country on foundations that will attract investment, raise the rates of growth, prevent monopoly and exploitation, protect workers, encourage manufacturing, increase exports, develop trade with the Arab world and the world in general, and in ways that serve our Palestinian interests and strengthen our self capacities, by issuing laws that are appropriate for all of this.

GRASSROOTS SOCIAL WORK

What is the role of Hamas at the grassroots level in Palestinian society?

Grassroots work has always been Hamas's strongest aspect. Its unstoppable rise over the past 20 years and eventual triumph over other Palestinian factions is largely attributed to its success in social work. This work takes the form of providing structured educational, health and welfare services and help to the poor. Through powerful pervasive networks of charities, mosques, unions, schools and sport clubs, Hamas's assistance and care of needy people have been felt personally by hundreds of thousands of Palestinians. The provision of these services has also been marked by honesty and transparency, which equally has always been compared with the corrupt performance of other major Palestinian factions, particularly Fatah, which controlled the Palestinian Authority from 1994. The popularity of Hamas and its victory in the 2006 elections is at least partially an outcome of its sustained devotion to helping the poor. Hamas was known to give monthly help even to people who worked for the Fatah Palestinian Authority when their income was considered to be below the poverty line.

Known to be Hamas's major strategic strength, the Islamic charities and institutions run by the movement have always been targeted by Israel. For years Israeli attacks aimed to close down these charities, block their funds and mobilize international campaigns against their external donors. Israel has tried to claim that Hamas's social work organizations in the West Bank and the Gaza Strip channel funds to Hamas's military activities. However, the real intention behind the continuous harassment and closure of these charities and facilities, either by Israel or later by the Palestinian Authority, was the popularity they bring to Hamas.

After 9/11 the pressure on Hamas and its activities multiplied. Israel succeeded in mobilizing the United States and the United Kingdom to take measures against a number of Islamic organizations accused of sending funds to Hamas's charities. The United States also pressurized the Palestinian Authority to act against Hamas's social activities, which included providing monthly stipends to the families of 'martyrs' to the cause of liberation, such as suicide bombers. This particularly was seen as an indirect encouragement for the future recruitment of bombers, who would rest assured that their families would enjoy protection and support.

At various periods of time Hamas's social work was really hindered or crippled by Israeli or official Palestinian efforts, yet it would gather momentum again and resume its operations. In the years 2003/04 the Palestinian Authority yielded to Israeli/ American pressure and took harsh measures against Hamas's charities, including freezing the bank accounts of twelve charities in the West Bank and 38 in the Gaza Strip. The Islamic Society, which has nine branches in the Gaza Strip, was a particular target. Protesting against these measures, thousands of Palestinian families took to the street in November 2003, throwing stones at the premises of the Legislative Council. According to local field workers, there were 120,000 Palestinians receiving monthly financial help from those charities. Thirty thousand more benefit from them on an annual basis.

Closing those charities did not help in either lessening
Hamas's military attacks, or reducing its popularity. Despite all
the ruthless measures against them, not only by Israel but also by
the Palestinian Authority, these charitable organizations remained
functioning, serving hundreds of thousands of poor Palestinians
in the Gaza Strip and the West Bank.

At one point, there was a remarkable show of power by
Hamas against the combined efforts of Israel, the United States
and the Palestinian Authority to block Hamas's funds. Hamas
wanted to show that it could solicit funds from ordinary Palestinians to support its organizational and military activities, and
that it did not need to rely on its impounded funds, nor would
any international blockade against external sources of funding
destroy it. Thus, it organized a one-day fundraising campaign in
the Gaza Strip on Friday, 9 April 2004. During and after Friday
prayers Hamas appealed to the Gazans to donate to the movement and specifically to its Izzedin al-Qassam military wing
(not to any outfit or charity affiliated to it). Canvassing all the
mosques and public places across the Gaza Strip, Hamas
collected huge sums of money. According even to independent
local sources, around US$1.2 million was estimated to have
been collected on that day. Hamas's own estimate was more
than double that figure.

*Does Hamas's social programme include imposing Islamic
symbols such as the* hijab *and other notions of* sharia *law on
the Palestinians?*

Ironically, within the sphere of Hamas's social work – its most
powerful strategic asset – lies one of the weakest aspects of the
movement: its heavily religious societal outlook. As was
discussed in Chapter 2, Hamas is a blend of liberation movement
and religious party. The religious drive within Hamas is indeed
visible and powerful, prompting many Palestinians to ask
whether the movement would be willing to impose its own views

and understanding of Islam on Palestinian society in the event of taking power.

Hamas's often-declared position is that it will never impose any religious practice on the Palestinians. Addressing detailed questions about the movement's stance regarding the *hijab*, alcohol, segregation between males and females and applying certain aspects of *sharia* law, Hamas's spokespersons are unanimous in negating the possibility of Hamas imposing such things on the Palestinians against their will. However there is a social dynamism and reality in the West Bank, and even more evident in the Gaza Strip, that reflects indirect practices or influences that contradict these official declarations. Because of the heavy presence of Hamas and the efficiency of its social activities, an atmosphere exists which has to some degree precipitated the indirect imposition of Hamas's norms on the Palestinians they support and help. Receiving continuous help and teaching from Hamas, many poor Palestinians would not only give their votes to Hamas in any coming elections, but in many cases would also adhere to the religious traditions and practice propagated by Hamas. And this does not simply follow out of gratitude or agreement. An unveiled woman for example would not think to apply for help from Hamas before veiling herself. This could be considered to be an indirect 'benign or paternal' imposition of practices.

More worrying examples surface, from time to time, of more 'malignant' impositions of practices. These include very direct and harsh interference by Hamas members against certain behaviour or events that are deemed 'immoral' in their eyes (partying, drinking alcohol, not wearing the *hijab*, mixed swimming and so forth). One infamous incident of this kind, which greatly embarrassed Hamas, was the murder of a Palestinian woman in her fiancé's car at the beach in Gaza in April by Hamas gunmen, and the beating up of her fiancé until he bled. Although Hamas condemned the incident and compensated the family of the woman, the justification provided by her killers was based on 'moral reasons and the fight against corruption'.

Hamas is still grappling with the idea of using power and influence to impose a 'religious moral code'. The more power and popularity the movement acquires, the more tempted it is to use its leverage to impose its social and religious ideals. There is visible confusion about Hamas's exploitation of its 'popular and political capital' on the 'religious morality' front. Some of Hamas's figures would convey the message with conviction that Hamas has the right to invest its 'resistance capital' in empowering an ideological social (or religious or cultural) vision on society. Not all Hamas supporters agree with its religious outlook. Palestinian society at large is very diverse, with secular and religious people, Muslims and Christians who have been living side by side for centuries without adhering to any rigid form of social or religious structure.

The potential misuse by Hamas of its 'resistance capital' in the religion/morality stakes is rooted in its self-perception of the role it has played. There is a valid claim made by Hamas that it has helped diminish certain negative phenomena in Palestinian society, such as the use of drugs, as well as its considerable contribution to social services and aid to thousands of poverty-stricken families. Yet this has often been in tandem with propagating ideas like the sorting of the social fabric into 'moral' and 'immoral' classifications. Such potentially inflexible or divisive classification in the Palestinian case, and in any resistance situation, only complicates matters and makes things more dangerous, and pushes the national movement away from its all-inclusive character.

There is tension here between what pertains to 'resistance' and what concerns 'society'. Hamas is facing the same choice that many movements before it have done, of linking its social agenda (the Islamization of society) with its resistance programme. It should acknowledge that achieving the former goal might result in the loss of the latter. The experience of the broader Palestinian national movement shows that a pluralist national and social approach, which includes different moderate versions of religiosity, is the most successful in mobilizing the widest sections of the Palestinian people.

In the months that followed Hamas's control of the Palestinian Authority in March 2006, the confusion within Hamas's government on where to start and where to stop on 'imposing' moral religiosity is still apparent. The ministers of culture, media and women's affairs (all members of Hamas) have made scattered statements on issues that could involve 'moral imposition' and censorship, such as movies and the contents of plays and other material. However, it is early yet to build an accurate view on Hamas's government performance on this issue.

What is the position of Hamas on women?

Hamas is no different from other mainstream Islamic movements whose ideas and practices with regard to women draw on the experience and thought of the Muslim Brotherhood. This means adhering to a conservative outlook on women. It is an outlook that is not as narrow-minded and rigid as that of fundamentalist extreme groups such as the Taliban of Afghanistan and the Salfis of Saudi Arabia. But at the same time it is not particularly open-minded, nor does it match the levels of freedom and achievements that are realized by women in many Arab and Muslim countries. Specifically, women in the Hamas movement are politically active especially in universities and graduate sectors (with syndications of engineers, doctors and so forth). They have their own committees at local and national level, with their main areas of interest being the rather traditional spheres of women, charities and schools. Hamas's female activism reaches high peaks at the time of elections, when female members of Hamas are fully mobilized to reach out to Palestinian women and attract their votes. Whether these elections take place at the level of student unions or parliament, the power of the 'female voters' is paramount to putting Hamas in the lead. Thus, women are very central to Hamas at the level of functioning in the field and mobilization: that is to say, for Hamas's own political interests.

At other levels, mainly leadership, in Hamas women disappear. Since it was founded in 1987 not a single female has been elevated to a political leadership position, barring the late appointment in March 2006 of Myriam Saleh to Hamas's cabinet as (rather predictably) minister of women's affairs. The female membership of Hamas consists mostly of university graduates who were active in their university years, but have been sidelined after marriage and family life. Their role is limited to familial and social affairs that are bound by geographical areas. Compared with the broader Palestinian national movement, where many female figures have left a political impact at the public and leadership level, Hamas's women are almost invisible to the outside world.

The widely believed conviction amongst Hamas's male membership is that the responsibility of women is mainly to look after home and family affairs. This view is popular as a matter of preference, but not as a dictat that could prohibit active women from pursuing other paths in their life. Hamas women work in schools, hospitals, companies, the media and other sectors. But they stop short of pursuing leading positions and avoid competing with men at those levels.

Within the 'resistance project' against the Israeli occupation, Hamas women play a significant mobilization role. They provide logistic and emotional support to the youth, and the mothers show a startling level of steadfastness when their boys are killed by the Israeli army. A very limited number of females from Hamas have carried out suicide attacks. Hamas leaders, ever adopting the 'benign paternal authority role', insist that they are not short of men to carry out these attacks.

When Hamas ran for the Palestinian parliamentary elections in the year 2006, it had on its list 13 females out of 66 candidates, with seven of them ending up winning contested seats. When

Hamas formed a Palestinian government by virtue of winning the majority, it only included one woman in the cabinet, Myriam Saleh. To the disappointment of many Hamas supporters who were hoping that the movement would show more openness, the portfolio that was assigned to Saleh was the ministry of women's affairs, a step that in effect perpetuates the traditional view that women's affairs are separate and should be administered by women.

In more than one way, Saleh's credentials which recommended her to that post reflect the profile of many of Hamas's women: young educated females who divide their time between family responsibilities and organizational activism. Saleh holds a doctorate in Islamic studies and taught at Palestinian universities for years prior to assuming her new job. Married with seven children, she is a devout mother, yet very engaged in Hamas activities: she is the founder and head of several women's organizations in the West Bank. In her view, 'women represent not only half of society, but actually its foundation'. Responding to questions about whether the Hamas government will impose the *hijab* (a garment covering the full body and head) on Palestinian women, she said:

> We assure all women that we will not force anybody to wear the *hijab* … we only present our ideas by suggestion and with good intention. The majority of Palestinian women wear the *hijab* with full conviction and without coercion from anyone.

6 Hamas and the Palestinians

HAMAS'S POPULARITY

How popular is Hamas in the West Bank and Gaza Strip?

Hamas's landslide victory in the 2006 Palestinian Legislative Council (PLC) elections shows a clear measure of its popularity. The movement's election Platform for Change and Reform, along with four independent candidates supported by Hamas, reaped almost 60 per cent of the votes, with a turnout of 78 per cent of eligible voters. The victory stunned everyone, including Hamas members themselves. Yet, when scrutinized at a deeper level, the share of votes that Hamas won far exceeds Hamas's real power, and it merits closer analysis.

Over the many years prior to the 2006 PLC elections Hamas's results in all kinds of elections, including those of student unions, professional associations and municipalities, averaged between 35 and 45 per cent. The ups and downs in the number of votes given to Hamas at various times corresponded to the political environment at the time of the particular elections. When people have been more hopeful of movement in peace talks with Israel, Hamas's 'programme for resistance' tended to generate more doubt, and a drop in Hamas supporters followed. By contrast, when frustration with fruitless talks has been mounting and exacerbated by continuous Israeli humiliation of Palestinians, in such a charged atmosphere Hamas has tended to gain more support in any elections held. The level of frustration and anger among the Palestinian electorate at the time of the 2006 PLC elections was unprecedented. The conjunction of unstoppable Israeli arrogance and military aggression against the Palestinians, coupled with the failure of the corrupt Fatah-led Palestinian Authority, furnished Hamas with the extra support that was added to its original hardcore constituency.

Therefore, the 60 per cent victory that Hamas achieved in the PLC elections was not reflective of its clear-cut strength, but rather represented a coming together of two separate voting segments, what might be called 'genuine support' and 'conditional support'. Hamas's solid genuine popularity is the constant support that it enjoys regardless of the fluctuations of the political situation, either at the level of the conflict with Israel or in internal Palestinian affairs. The bedrock popularity of Hamas ranges between 30 per cent and 40 per cent of the entire Palestinian constituency. Any additional support to this share comes effectively from the conjunction of public reaction against the blunders and failures of Hamas's rivals, public frustration or outrage at ongoing humiliations from Israel, and most unforgivably, corruption within.

This assessment of Hamas's support was somewhat confirmed four months after its PLC election victory, when it had to face the first critical test regarding its popularity. Hamas supporters ran for the student union elections of Bir Zeit University, the biggest and most politicized Palestinian higher education institution in the West Bank. Historically, Bir Zeit University has been the stronghold of secular and leftist Palestinian groups. From the early 1990s Hamas started to fiercely contest the leadership of the student union. In April 2006 elections in an intensified electoral battle against the Fatah platform, Hamas won a majority of 23 seats out of the 51 being contested on the student council, leaving Fatah with only 18 seats, with the remaining ten divided among other factions. Hamas's Bir Zeit victory of 45 per cent of the votes is a much more accurate indicator of Hamas's real power on the ground than the inflated 60 per cent of the 2006 PLC victory, and is historically consistent as well.

> *How much influence does Hamas have among the 5 million Palestinians who live outside Palestine (in the Arab world, Europe and the United States)?*

Unlike the situation in the West Bank and the Gaza Strip, there has been little visible presence of Hamas within the Palestinian communities abroad, barring the refugee camps in Lebanon and Syria. Although this situation could change after Hamas's victory in the PLC elections, it is certainly difficult to draw an accurate assessment of Hamas's 'outside' popularity. There have been few electoral processes outside Palestine with Hamas-affiliated groups partaking whose results could offer reliable indications of Hamas support and influence amongst Palestinians worldwide.

In general, the political orientations of the expat Palestinian communities vary according to their place and conditions of residence. Tentatively, it could be said that the closer to Palestine and the harder the living conditions for a Palestinian community, the more supportive to Hamas it could be. Also, the more the Palestinians who live in various countries are exposed to the influences of local Islamist movements, the more support they tend to show to Hamas. Thus, Hamas is notably popular in the refugee camps in Lebanon, Syria and Jordan. These are the places closest to Palestine, where not only is the daily 'hot news from home' followed in detail, but also these countries themselves unavoidably feel the pressures of the conflict constantly. In Jordan, in particular, where the majority of the population is Palestinian or of Palestinian origin, and the influence of Jordanian Islamists is paramount, Hamas's popularity matches the levels of the West Bank and Gaza Strip. As an indirect indicator, many Palestinians who are supposedly Hamas supporters typically vote for the Jordanian Muslim Brotherhood, whose average share of the Jordanian Parliamentary seats ranges between 30 and 35 per cent. The Palestine issue and support for the Palestinian struggle against Israel normally figure on the top of any electoral platform of the Jordanian Islamists.

By contrast, Palestinians who live in the United States, Europe and other places far from Palestine are relatively less supportive of Hamas. Yet again there is no concrete evidence that could be used to identify general trends for the extent to which those Palestinians support Hamas, or Fatah for that matter. Many Palestinians have been living in these areas well before the establishment of Hamas, leading secular and non-religious styles of life. It is safe to suggest that the observance of religious teachings, which is a pivotal underpinning in supporting Hamas, is visibly less in evidence among European and US–based Palestinians than among those who live in Palestine or the Arab countries. Thus, Hamas's popularity within the former communities lags behind its levels within the latter.

How much influence does Hamas have on Palestinians inside Israel proper?

Inside Israel proper, that is to say outside the West Bank and the Gaza Strip, there are about 1.2 million Palestinians, who represent about 25 per cent of the Israeli population. They remained on territory within what became the new Israeli borders during and after the 1948 war, and officially became Israeli citizens. Largely displaced from their original homes and villages, these Palestinians managed to resettle in less desirable areas within Israel, and have since suffered much discrimination, in spite of their nominal citizenship status. In terms of level of education, achievement, careers and freedoms they lag behind the bulk of Israeli society. Their inherent allegiance has always been questioned and they have been seen by the Israeli establishment as a 'fifth column', working for the enemy. Their identity has been torn between officially being citizens of the state of Israel which was established on their own land, and their own 'Palestinianism'. Prevented from serving in the army or assuming high-ranking positions in the government, the 'Arabs of Israel', as they are usually called, have never been given the same privileges as other Israelis in relation to their political, linguistic and legal rights. Israelis look at them with deep suspicion. However, Palestinians everywhere consider them part and parcel of the Palestinian people. They live in almost exclusively 'Palestinian' cities and villages, with little mixing with the larger Jewish population.

Other than a minority of Israeli-Palestinians who have joined major Israeli parties, the politically active members of this community have created their own parties, spanning leftist, nationalist and Islamist leanings. These parties compete against each other in local municipalities to represent and defend the rights of Palestinians in Israel on legal grounds and without the use of violence. Since the mid-1980s, a strong Islamist movement has spawned within the 'Israeli Arabs', challenging all the other Arab parties. This took place almost in tandem with the emergence of Hamas in the West Bank and the Gaza Strip. The religious affinity between these movements is definitely strong, but they operate differently. The leaders and members of the 'Islamist movement' in Israel function in Israel within Israeli law, but Hamas functions in the West Bank and Gaza and is against Israel altogether. There are no organizational links between the two.

The 'Islamist movement' in Israel is morally and politically supportive of Hamas. During the 1980s and 1990s it was accused of being active in channelling funds to charities affiliated with Hamas. Hamas's appeal and activities have rained mixed fortunes on the 'Islamist movement'. On the one hand, Hamas has inspired its members to mobilize more strongly against the Israeli authorities, and to strengthen the 'Islamist' ideals within their constituencies. On the other hand, Hamas's suicide attacks in Israeli cities, killing civilians, have greatly affected them negatively, since, caught in the crossfire both figuratively and at times literally, they have felt unable to support Hamas publicly. At the high peak of the suicide bombings, leaders of both wings of the Islamist movement, which had by then split into two, publicly condemned Hamas's operations.

By and large, Hamas has little political leverage either on the 'Islamist movement' in Israel or on the overall Palestinian constituency there. Supporting Hamas would bring down heavy security and legal bearings upon the Arabs of Israel, thus even any emotional support they might offer is almost hidden. The most that Hamas can aspire to get from the Islamists inside Israel is support for its charities and campaigning against the deArabization of Jerusalem. Because these Islamists and the Arabs of Israel in general are official Israelis, they can move in and out Jerusalem freely, thus they are able to mobilize themselves to protest about Israeli measures to eradicate the Arab nature and places of the city.

HAMAS AND SECULAR PALESTINIAN MOVEMENTS

What is Hamas's view of and relationship with the Palestine Liberation Organization?

The PLO was established in the mid-1960s and has since evolved to embody the Palestinian national movement. It is a secular umbrella of all Palestinian factions, left, right and centre, with the Fatah movement being its backbone and leading force. Established before the 1967 war and the fall of the West Bank and the Gaza Strip to Israeli occupation, the PLO was originally created to 'liberate Palestine': that is, the land on which Israel was formed after the 1948 war. Yet by the early 1980s the aim of the PLO became to liberate the West Bank and the Gaza Strip, and establish a Palestinian state with implicit acknowledgement of the state of Israel. In 1988 the PLO recognized Israel, and in the following years from 1991 to 1993 it engaged in peace talks with Israel in the hope of realizing its 'new' aim of a Palestinian state. When the Palestinian Authority was established on Palestinian territories according to the Oslo Accords, the PLO officially became the ultimate representative of all Palestinians inside and outside Palestine (especially since the status of refugees remained unresolved). However the Palestinian Authority only deals with the Palestinians in the West Bank and Gaza Strip.

Hamas was bound to compete with the PLO since its emergence in 1987. It rejected the 'secular' nature of the organization and condemned its continuous concessions to Israel. In contrast to the later PLO conviction that Palestinian goals would only ultimately be realized through a negotiated settlement with Israel, Hamas advocated a resistance approach, which was justified all along the way by the obvious futility of the peace talks. Because of the secularity of the PLO and its 'capitulating' approach as perceived by Hamas, Hamas refused to join the PLO. Because of its immovabilty on this point, Hamas has always been accused of functioning at a distance from the collective national effort, and thus harming it. Not only that, it has been accused of undermining the PLO by not recognizing it as the sole and legitimate representative of the Palestinian people. Because the PLO fought hard against regional players, such as Israel, Jordan and Syria, to exact the status of 'the sole and legitimate representative of the Palestinians', it accused Hamas of indirectly undermining Palestinian legitimacy and representation.

Hamas, for its part, was inflexible on the issue of recognizing the PLO as the sole representative of the Palestinians. The most that it would acknowledge was that the PLO is 'a representative', not 'the representative', of the Palestinian people. Hamas also suggested that it might join the PLO if it was represented by 40–50 per cent of the PLO leading hierarchy. Hamas has continued to express its readiness to discuss joining the PLO, yet it has put forward terms completely unacceptable to Fatah, the central force of the PLO.

The Fatah movement has been fully aware of the challenge that Hamas has represented. As the PLO/Fatah continued its peace talks approach, almost from 1988 onward Hamas has travelled alongside with its 'resistance' approach. With the continuous erosion of PLO legitimacy because of the lack of success of the peace talks route, Hamas became more powerful and intractable in its rejection of joining the PLO. Finally, in 2005 Hamas and Fatah along with other Palestinian factions agreed on the principle of restructuring the PLO so that Hamas could join.

When Hamas won the elections of 2006 it dealt the greatest blow to Fatah and the PLO, this time challenging the status of 'the sole and legitimate representative of the Palestinian people' as it had never been challenged before. In its cabinet platform, Hamas refused, once again, to recognize the sole legitimacy and representation of the PLO, infuriating Fatah and many other Palestinians who have argued that the PLO is above factional rivalry. Hamas, however, was eager to form a national unity government and called upon Fatah, other factions and independent members of the newly elected parliament to join. They all rebuffed Hamas's offer because of its position on the PLO.

Will Hamas's rivalry with the Fatah movement end with an inevitable Palestinian civil war?

The rivalry between Hamas and Fatah has brought the Palestinians to the verge of civil war at various points between 1994 and 2000. Hamas's leaders, especially Sheikh Ahmad Yasin, were vehemently against such a development, and many Palestinians give them the credit for absorbing and defusing much of the provocations and suppression that Hamas faced from Fatah and the Palestinian Authority. The major issue that drove both parties to intense friction was Hamas's persistence in carrying on its military attacks against Israeli targets at times when the Fatah-led Palestinian Authority was trying to conclude incremental peace deals with Israel. Hamas's armed wing was seen by the Palestinian Authority as an uncontrolled group with illegitimate arms, which should be brought under the authority of the Palestinian security forces created by the Palestinian Authority.

In the post-2006 election period and with Hamas becoming the Palestinian Authority, Fatah attempted to bring down Hamas's government and started to play the role that Hamas used to play when it was in the opposition. While Hamas was anxious to buy time and bring calm to the Gaza Strip and the West Bank so that it could prove itself as a successful government, Fatah became the spoiler that Hamas had been in the past. The military wings of Fatah have always been difficult to control even by the Fatah leadership itself. With large stocks of arms and separate armed groups which move chaotically without clear focus and aims, the possibility of the Palestinian situation drifting into civil war is becoming higher than ever before.

What is Hamas's view of and relationship with the Palestinian left?

The left wing has a long and nostalgic history in Palestine, with the first Communist Palestinian party being established in Jaffa in the 1920s. It also had a pioneering role in inspiring parts of the Arab left movement in general. In the decades after the establishment of Israel in 1948, especially during the 1960s and 1970s, the Palestinian left was in the forefront of the struggle. Its relationships with the Palestinian Islamists and the Muslim Brotherhood during those decades were extremely bad. The Islamists were seen as a backward social force which contributed nothing to the struggle against Israel. When Hamas was formed in the late

1980s, the Palestinian left was confused about whether to welcome the sudden decision by the Islamists (in the guise of Hamas) to become engaged in active confrontation with Israel, or to fear their definitely rising power.

Against this backdrop of historical suspicion and lack of common ideological ground, Hamas and the Palestinian left organizations developed rather limited relationships. They were mainly propelled by a collective rejection of Fatah's (and the PLO's) willingness to participate in the Madrid Peace Conference in 1991, and then in the Oslo Agreements of 1993/4. Hamas and other Palestinian factions formed an alliance against Fatah, and fanned the flames of the spontaneous people's *intifada* in progress as the resistance alternative to the Fatah 'capitulating' approach. This alliance never came to the stage of issuing joint statements, and stopped short of any concrete joint political or military actions. Intrinsically, the Palestinian left rejected the 'religious content' of Hamas, and kept pressing for more secular emphasis in the struggle against Israel. In the end, suspicion and ideological differences overrode common cause and pragmatism.

One of the major issues that have kept Hamas and the Palestinian left apart has always been Hamas's unreserved refusal to recognize the PLO as the sole representative of the Palestinian people, as discussed above. The leftist organizations thought that this constant rejection revealed Hamas's future intention to exclusively control the Palestinian leadership. For its part, Hamas despaired of the left because whenever and wherever Hamas clashed on the ground with Fatah, the left would either stay neutral or implicitly support Fatah. Hamas has felt that the left have been hypocritical, only paying lip service to an alliance with Hamas against the political capitulation of Fatah. For its part, the left has always accused Hamas of short-sightedness and engaging in unnecessary political battles or field provocations.

After the elections of January 2006, Hamas's relationship

with the Palestinian left have further deteriorated. None of the three small leftist groups which won seven seats in total in the PLC agreed to join Hamas's government. Hamas blamed them for foiling its efforts to form a national coalition government.

In March 2006, Mousa Abu Marzouq, Hamas's deputy head of its Political Bureau, publicly criticized the Democratic Popular Front for the Liberation of Palestine (DPF) for its refusal to join the government. He also predicted that this group would disappear completely from the Palestinian political scene if it did not acknowledge the 'new realities'. One of the 'new realities' that Marzouq was pointing out to the DPF was the 'Islamic choice' that the Palestinian people had made when they elected Hamas, a choice which contradicted the DPF demand that Hamas state clearly that one of its government's objectives would be to 'secularize Palestinian society'. Marzouq insisted that it was illogical of the DPF to put forward this demand when it had managed to get only one member elected to the parliament (out of 132), particularly in light of the fact that that Hamas itself, with its vast majority in parliament, had not called for the 'Islamization of Palestinian society'.

How has the Hamas/Fatah rivalry developed?

The general characteristic of relations between Fatah and Hamas ever since the latter was formed, and between Fatah and Hamas's mother organization prior to the emergence of Hamas, has been one of virtually continuous competition and tension. Fatah, the Palestinian National Liberation Movement, was formally established in 1965. The origins of the movement, however, predated that by almost a decade, with some of Fatah's roots partly branching out from the Muslim Brotherhood. Until the mid-1950s the Palestinian Muslim Brotherhood (PMB) in the Gaza Strip and to a lesser extent in the West Bank enjoyed considerable strength, emanating from the then powerful position of its mother organization in Egypt, which was ruled by the pan-Arabist leader Nasser. In the second half of the 1950s Nasser outlawed the Muslim Brothers in Egypt and mercilessly suppressed them not only in Egypt but also in the Gaza Strip, which was then under Egyptian administration in a similar manner as the West Bank was under Jordanian administration after the 1948 war. Prominent figures of the PMB decided to leave the organization, for it was seen to be heavily involved in an unnecessary struggle with Nasser, and they wished to create a movement whose entire focus would be the Palestine issue.

In July 1957 Khalil al-Wazir, an active PMB member (he would eventually become the second and long-standing leader of Fatah until his assassination by the Israelis in Tunis in 1988) presented a proposal to the leadership of the PMB in the Gaza Strip. In it al-Wazir suggested a new approach where:

> the Palestinian Brotherhood should establish a special organization alongside their own which has no visible Islamic coloration or agenda but which has the stated goal of liberating Palestine through armed struggle. The new organization should have the responsibility for preparing for that struggle and should engage in armed struggle once the required capabilities are acquired.
>
> ('Azza, 1992, pp. 85–6)

The PMB did not take Khalil al-Wazir's proposal seriously, but al-Wazir and his close colleagues went ahead with the project on their own initiative.

The effort of those former PMB members in the Gaza Strip was coordinated with other groups of active Palestinians (both pan-Arabists and nationalists, among others) outside Palestine who advocated a similar line of thinking, and Fatah was gradually in the making. The idea of Fatah was to disentangle the Palestinian national effort from inter-Arab rivalries by creating an ideology-free movement that would accept the membership and support of any party or individual who believed in 'the liberation of Palestine', without any additional ideological package. Over the next following years, initial Fatah cells succeeded in bringing together active Palestinians from different political backgrounds, including, of course, some former members of the PMB.

Soon after its formation, between its adoption of armed struggle as the only strategy to 'liberate Palestine', and its setting aside of all ideological differences and conflicts with 'reactionary' Arab regimes, Fatah rose to capture the imagination and support of the vast majority of Palestinians. By the end of the 1960s it was far ahead of any other leftist, pan-Arabist or Islamist Palestinian faction. Parallel to Fatah's rise, the PMB receded to the background, fearing Nasser's wrath and convincing itself that the Fatah project was hasty and doomed to failure. It watched the continuing ascendance of Fatah with envy and dismay; many of its leaders had to live with the harsh fact that a number of their juniors had become leaders of the new rival and more popular movement. In the PMB literature the 1950s defection of some of its members to take part in the creation of Fatah is treated with bitterness and confusion. Sometimes old leaders of the PMB would regret not having controlled Fatah from the outset instead of letting it grow away from their influence. In the 1970s and most of the 1980s the PMB was inactive on the front of fighting the Israeli occupation; instead it was preoccupied with a 'preparation strategy; a grass-roots process of Islamization of young generations that would be ready to fight Israel in the future' (see Chapter 1). During those 'idle years' Fatah accused the inactive PMB of merely serving the Israeli occupation.

As the PMB eventually transformed itself into Hamas in 1987, bringing with its change of stance a surprisingly swift increase in its strength, it entered into competition with Fatah for support at the Palestinian grass-roots level. The charges against the PMB/Hamas changed from fence-sitting to trying to create an alternative to the PLO and trying to unravel the achievements of the PLO and its mainstay, Fatah. In the early 1990s relations between the two factions deteriorated dramatically. One of the major arenas of conflict was inside the Israeli prisons, where Fatah and Hamas prisoners clashed bloodily. Hamas prisoners were not allowed by Fatah members who had been in prison much longer to form their own cell groups, and were forced to join the already existing 'system of grouping' which was exclusive to factions that belonged to the PLO. Thus Hamas inmates had to go through the educational and indoctrination courses organized by other factions, which naturally led to disputes on ideology and views. The prison clashes spread outside, and the atmosphere was charged in many Palestinian cities and refugee camps, until late in 1992 when the Fatah leadership agreed to give Hamas prisoners the right to form their own groups.

A new phase of rivalry came into being with the establishment of the Palestinian Authority (PA) in 1994, as a result of the Oslo Agreements of 1993. The Palestinian Authority, led by Fatah, was supposed to prove that it was competent to run an interim administration for a period of five years, after which negotiations between Israel and the Palestinian Authority would begin, establishing the 'permanent solution' and the creation of a Palestinian state. Fatah saw in the Agreement a chance to realize Palestinian rights, and concurrently stopped its armed struggle. Hamas, by contrast, saw the Agreement as a continuation of the Israeli occupation by proxy, and continued its armed struggle. The Palestinian Authority considered Hamas to be a spoiler, and demanded that the movement stop its military attacks against Israel so that peace talks could be given a chance. Hamas considered daily Israeli measures to essentially be ignoring the accords, as Israel continued not only its usual policies on the ground, but especially its relentless expansion of settlements. Thus the major issue that drove both parties to intense friction between 1994 and the year 2000 was Hamas's persistence in carrying on its military attacks against Israeli targets at times when the Fatah-led PA was trying to conclude incremental peace deals with Israel.

The second *intifada* of 2000 forced the two parties to downplay their differences and focus on the Israeli occupation and its incursions into Palestinian cities and refugee camps. Practically speaking, the Oslo Agreements had failed and Israel's brutal measures were imposed on Palestinian activists regardless of their organizational affiliation. Israel effectively reoccupied all the areas that it had initially (if only partly) withdrawn from according to the Oslo Agreement. The president of the Palestinian Authority, Yasser Arafat, was besieged in his offices in Ramallah for almost three years, from February 2002 until his death in October 2004. It was reported that Arafat extended indirect help to Hamas and turned a blind eye to the further arming of Hamas. The time around Arafat's death, marked the period of least friction between Fatah and Hamas in the past few years.

In the post-2006 election period when Hamas took the reins of the Palestinian Authority, Fatah attempted to bring down Hamas's government and started to play the role that Hamas used to play when it was in the opposition. While Hamas was anxious to buy time and bring calm to the Gaza Strip and the West Bank so that it could prove itself as a successful government, Fatah became the spoiler that Hamas had been in the past. The military wings of Fatah have always been difficult to control even by the Fatah leadership itself. With large stocks of arms and separate armed groups which move chaotically without clear focus and aims, the possibility of the Palestinian situation drifting into civil war was becoming higher than ever before. Eventually, the civil war nightmare scenario that many Palestinians had feared became reality in mid-June 2007. At that point, Hamas violently used force to seize power over all the security services that had continued to be controlled by Fatah. Many Palestinians were killed or injured in the clashes. Ultimately, Hamas won over Fatah militarily as it had democratically in the January 2006 elections (see Chapter 10).

What is Hamas's view of and relationship with Palestinian Christians?

In its conduct towards the Palestinian Christians Hamas has shown extraordinary sensitivity. Realizing that its views on non-Muslims and its dealing with them would always be brought under the spotlight because of Hamas's religious colouring, the movement has succeeded in establishing cordial relationships with Palestinian Christians. Bearing in mind that the vast majority of Palestinian Christians are quite secular in lifestyle, there have been in general few areas of potential friction with Hamas. It has been the convergences of nationalist cause, not the divergences of religious beliefs, that have governed the relationship.

In its official documents Hamas speaks with warmth about the sacrifices of the Palestinian Christians, who have shown steadfastness side by side with their Muslim counterparts in the face of the Israeli occupation and its atrocities. Hamas keeps referring with a deep sense of pride to the fact that Muslims and Christians and (pre-Israel) Jews have long lived in peaceful coexistence in Palestine, and Hamas would maintain that tradition. Also, the specificity of the Palestinian situation has compelled Hamas to adopt a consensual and cooperative approach towards other Palestinians regardless of their religious or political affiliation.

In actuality though, many Christians have felt uncomfortable with the increasing rise of Hamas. The religious atmosphere that is created alongside Hamas's political rise undoubtedly brings about a somewhat discomfiting climate for Christians, as well as for secular Muslims. There are some views and research which argue that the rise of Hamas in Palestine has put extra pressures on the Palestinian Christians, causing an increase in the rate of their migration abroad. But in general, there have been no religious-driven or sectarian friction or riots in Palestine during the lifetime of Hamas that could be linked directly to the movement.

Hamas's rivalry with other Palestinian groups has been almost exclusively politically driven. Its main concern has always been with the Fatah movement, which is predominantly Muslim. With the other two major, though smaller, groups – the Popular Front for the Liberation of Palestine and the Democratic Front for the Liberation of Palestine – Hamas has developed closer relationships, and both are headed by Christians. Indeed, this fact has never affected Hamas's position toward these two leftist factions.

In its 2006 election campaign for the PLC, Hamas supported two independent Christian candidates, one in Gaza and another in Bethlehem. When it had to form a cabinet, it included a Christian as one of its ministerial team. Although there are no organizational rules that prohibit a Christian from joining Hamas, the movement has failed to attract a single Christian to its membership. This failure embarrasses Hamas as it is the only Palestinian movement whose membership is exclusively based on Muslims, though not by dictat but by practical reality.

7 Hamas and 'International Islamism'

HAMAS AND MUSLIM COUNTRIES

What are Hamas's relationships with other Arab and Muslim countries?

Hamas's relationships with different Arab and Muslim countries vary from one country to another depending on various factors. These relationships exist at two levels; at the cautious official level and at the (usually) warm and more supportive popular level. In the Arab region, states that are known to have an outspoken, strong policy line against Israel, even if only verbally, are naturally closer to Hamas. This group includes Iran, Syria, Sudan, Lebanon and Libya, where Hamas has succeeded in establishing official links and has its own offices. Iran figures at the top of this group, openly supporting Hamas politically and financially, with Hamas enjoying almost full diplomatic status in Tehran. In the other countries, Hamas has offices and spokespersons and operates at the political and media level.

Another group of states includes Egypt and the Gulf states, Saudi Arabia, Qatar and Kuwait. These countries are well known for their non-revolutionary politics but they attempt to maintain a reasonable relationship with Hamas in order to counterbalance what is perceived to be the somewhat threatening Iranian/Syrian influence on Hamas. Egypt is particularly keen to have strong links with Hamas, and has mediated several times since the late 1990s between Hamas and Israel to reach a 'truce'. Egypt's interest is in having calm and security in the bordering Gaza Strip, and to keep the rise of Palestinian Islamism under check so that it does not spill over Egyptian borders. A third group of countries includes reluctant countries who quietly consider Hamas to be a source of threat to their domestic affairs and thus an unwelcome presence on their land. Jordan and the Maghreb countries, such as Tunisia, Algeria and Morocco, could be considered among this group.

Beyond the Arab region, Hamas has established varying levels of links with Pakistan, Malaysia, Indonesia and Turkey. Delegations from Hamas make frequent visits to these countries to appeal to their 'Muslim brothers' for support for Palestine and for Hamas. Governments of these countries have established calculated links with Hamas in order to make sure that Hamas's contacts in their countries are not taking place behind the back of the regime. The principal concern in most Arab and Muslim countries is to monitor Hamas and its contacts and extract the guarantee from the movement that it will have no activities in the country, and will only be a receiver of support and not become an inspiration or mobilizer of any disgruntled factions there. However, in the cases of Malaysia and Turkey Hamas enjoys considerable contact and looks with high appreciation to the moderate Islamist ruling parties there.

In all countries Hamas's eye has always been on nurturing strong relationships and presence among the people, through the political parties and Islamic associations. The wider Hamas strategy is based on engaging Arab and Muslim peoples in supporting the Palestinians. Reaching out to these particular populations is vital, for it explains the Palestinian suffering and solicits support in moral, political and financial forms. At the official level, Hamas has focused on acquiring political and diplomatic recognition and legitimacy. Hamas has been very keen to be accepted as a political organization that is received and respected by governments, so that it constantly tries to mitigate its image as a 'terrorist organization'. Official links also help in enhancing Hamas's aspiration of representing the Palestinians and speaking for them, against the wishes of the PLO, the officially recognized body for that purpose.

At the popular level, Hamas has succeeded in creating strong local relationships with Islamist parties, associations and individuals. Not only within the realm of Islamists, but also within the anti-Israeli and anti-American camps, Hamas has enjoyed warm relationships and support. These relationships have played a fundamental role in helping Hamas in fundraising and mobilization of public opinion in the Arab and Muslim world. Supporters of Hamas will convey its message and defend its views and practices in their areas, by political and media means. The sympathy for Hamas in the Gulf and other Arab and Muslim countries often reaches high levels, creating the much-needed atmosphere in which Hamas's local supporters, organizations or individuals, are able to collect considerable funds for the movement.

HAMAS AND MUSLIM COMMUNITIES IN THE WEST

What has been the impact of Hamas's rise on the growing number of Islamist movements in the world, especially in the West?

In the general realm of Muslims worldwide, Hamas's rise as an Islamist Palestinian movement has encouraged millions of Muslims to further support the cause of Palestine. Muslim communities in the West are no exception. Palestine occupies a central and emotional place in the imagination and sentiment of Muslims. Hamas believes that with the adoption of a strong Islamic ideology, an additional level of power will be bestowed upon the call for support of the Palestinians. Ordinary Muslims would certainly feel more resonance with the Islamist discourse of Hamas than the secular discourse of the PLO. With the spread of Islamic political movements in the past three decades, Muslim communities in the West have become amenable to Hamas's call in particular. What Hamas has most wanted from them has been the propagation of the Palestine cause and funding of Hamas's charitable work. Almost simultaneously with the eruption of the first *intifada* in late 1987, many Islamic organizations were established in Europe and the United States in order to help the affected Palestinians. Money poured into Islamic charities that were efficiently run by Hamas. Hamas reaped the fruits and amassed further popularity.

In more specific areas, Hamas influences Islamist movements worldwide by offering a '*jihad* model' that is not controversial by nature of its just cause, but would not hesitate to use controversial means to serve that cause. Hamas's *jihad* is seen as directed against Israel, a foreign military occupation led by Zionist Jews against Muslim homelands and holy places. Because this particular *jihad* is not launched against a contentious Muslim regime or despised government where Muslims would end up fighting Muslims, there is a near consensus among Islamists everywhere on the righteousness and justice of Hamas's struggle. Also, Hamas is considered to be a source of inspiration – an example of steadfastness in the face of tremendous pressures – because of its committed refusal to bow to the status quo and international forces and recognize Israel, as the PLO did.

On the other hand, Hamas's controversial means, specifically the suicide attacks, have also influenced many Islamists and propelled many of them into adopting this tactic. Although they were originally introduced into modern conflicts in the Middle East by Shiat militants in Lebanon in 1982, against US-led multinational troops, suicide bombings had to wait until the early 1990s before they were freely adopted by Hamas. Despite the justifications made by Hamas to legitimize this controversial practice (see Chapter 4), the movement bears the responsibility for having promoted this kind of self-killing amongst modern Islamists as a manner of inflicting maximum harm on the side of the enemy. It could be said that the waves of suicide bombings conducted by radical Islamist groups across the globe in the 1990s and 2000s have been mostly inspired by Hamas's conduct.

The activities of Hamas's supporters in the West have been restricted to informational, political and financial support. There purposefully has never been any military or armed action outside Palestine. Hamas has been vigorously strict on avoiding any direct or indirect engagement in armed activities in the West, or encouraging or approving any action in that direction undertaken by its supporters. As a result of this, many US and European judicial cases against organizations and individuals close to Hamas and charged with 'sponsoring the terrorism of Hamas' have failed. These organizations had been channelling money to thousands of poor Palestinians via Islamist charities that were associated to Hamas. All money transfers from the United States or Europe were undertaken via Western or Israeli banks, under the full monitoring of Western and Israeli intelligence as to where this money came from and to whom it was given. Hamas and its supporters abroad have been successful in maintaining a complete distance between the political, social and financial funding of the movement and its military branch and activities.

Is there either a visible or invisible presence of Hamas in the West?

There is no organizational structure for Hamas in the West. It has been felt that any such remote structure with any degree of party-strictness, however loyal it might be, would add an extra unnecessary burden on the movement in return for benefits that it already receives through the existing system of supporters.

Thus, until the formation of Hamas's government in 2006, there was no official spokesperson or address for Hamas in any western country. In short, there had been no visible presence. Yet, as outlined above, there has been an 'indirect' presence through Islamist networks and associations in the West that have shown support and solidarity to Hamas either directly or indirectly by virtue of their broader support of the Palestine question. Many of these associations have been established by Palestinians who are driven emotionally and politically to support their people. Within these circles of Western expat Palestinian societies and communities, more visible support for Hamas can undoubtedly be found.

What matters most, in an atmosphere charged by suspicion about Muslims and Arabs in the West, is that Hamas's invisibility in the West does not mean that it has an underground cellular network, armed or unarmed. Since it was established in 1987 and up to the present there has not been a single incident where Hamas was proved to have operated any illegal action within or against any Western country or citizens. The eagerness that Hamas has always shown about having a future presence in the West was specifically directed to, and restricted to, the establishment of official contacts with western governments. Succeeding on that front has always borne far more strategic significance for Hamas than recruiting individuals or setting up underground cells.

HAMAS AND ISLAMIST MOVEMENTS

Is Hamas part of a global network of 'international Islamism'?

The immediate answer to the question whether Hamas constitutes part of a global network of 'international Islamism', is yes – and no. If by 'international Islamism' we mean a coherent organizational structure, where various groups and parties worldwide belong to a single and unified 'umbrella' hierarchy, then the answer is no. If, however, the term denotes a loose common ground where Islam is considered the source of ideological convictions and guidelines, then the answer is yes.

Perhaps against the conventional thinking of many in the West, Islamist movements differ startlingly, one from another. First of all there are political movements and nonpolitical movements. The latter type of movement is hardly mentioned, as these function quietly and limit their efforts to charitable work, religious preaching and propagation of the call to Islam But the other type, known as movements of political Islam, constitute a rising force not only in the Middle Eastern context, but globally.

Even within those groups affiliated to political Islam, the factors that separate them from each other perhaps override those that unite them. Some movements are engaged in fierce and armed conflict against their governments and are confined within their national boundaries. Their *jihad* aims to bring down these governments, which are seen as unIslamic, and to replace them with Islamic ones. Democratic means are rejected by these groups because they imply recognition of the non-Islamic status quo under which democracy is implemented. Examples of such political Islam groups exist in Algeria, Egypt and Pakistan, yet they are not the mainstream Islamists.

Other movements conduct their protests against the ruling elites in their countries by peaceful means, and in many cases through parliamentary political processes. The main groups in this category are the Muslim Brotherhoods that exist almost in every Arab or Muslim country. These groups abandon the use of violence altogether, and prefer long and patient incremental reform within the system. Each group operates within the nation-state boundaries of its country.

Another generation of more recent and radical Islamist groups is 'stateless' in terms of the focus of their *jihad*. This means they are not bound to the confines of any certain country, and consider the very existence of many Muslim states as an abnormality to the 'supposed' one and unified single Muslim country. These groups are the force behind 'global *jihad*', where fighting is driven by the injustices suffered by Muslims, and against those who inflict these injustices, regardless of time and space. The West in general and the United States in particular is the number one enemy to this type of Islamist movement. Thus, western interests in Arab and Muslim countries and elsewhere are their legitimate targets. Instead of fighting puppet leaders and governments installed by the West to maintain its interests in the region, they advocate that the fight be launched directly against the West, the principal culprit. 'By attacking the head, the tail falls off,' these factions are fond of repeating.

Within this mishmash of Islamist movements, Hamas is somehow unique. Its fight is not against any national regime, but against colonial foreign occupation. Its national liberation substance is no less potent than its religious creed (see Chapter 2). In many cases, and within the realm of 'international Islamism,' Hamas's nationalist concerns have overridden its religious affinities. One recent and unmistakable example was its dismissal of calls from its 'Chechen brothers' to cancel an official visit of a Hamas delegation to Moscow in February 2006. For the Chechens, the Russian leadership is criminal and guilty of killing thousands of Muslims in the 1994 war against Chechnya. Hamas, it was felt, as an Islamist brotherly organization should never shake hands with the criminals. Hamas dismissed this and thought that fostering relations with Moscow had far more value to the Palestine issue than showing solidarity with its Chechen brothers.

In conclusion, the concept of 'international Islamism' stops far short of any effective and concerted plan of action. It is only manifested in verbal solidarity, moral and perhaps material support, but does not amount to a coherent global force that would have any particular significance to Hamas.

What is the difference between Hamas and al-Qaeda, and is there any cooperation between the two?

There are big differences between the two movements, in terms of the ends, means and battlefield, and also the nature of each movement. Because of such differences, Hamas is indeed very anxious to keep itself well distanced from al-Qaeda, and certainly does not engage in any cooperation with it. If we compare the 'ends' of both these organizations, Hamas's aims are focused. They began with the 'liberation of Palestine' then narrowed down later and refocused on ending the Israeli occupation of the West Bank and Gaza Strip. Al-Qaeda's ends are almost the reverse in type: vague and without focus, and expanding, with the ultimate goal being to establish Islamic rule over Arab and Muslim lands after ridding them of foreign troops and puppet leaders. They also include intermediate goals such as forcing American troops to leave Arabian land, fighting US and British armies in Afghanistan and Iraq, and bringing down puppet governments in the Gulf countries and elsewhere. All along the way, al-Qaeda would implement a very strict interpretation of Islamic practices on any area and segment of any population it would come to control, with the Taliban 'model' as its ideal.

To realize its end, Hamas is engaged in a 'resistance programme' which includes armed struggle and political conduct. Within its armed struggle it has adopted the controversial tactic of suicide attacks, justified by the Old Testament as 'an eye for an eye', a stance that has currency it has to be said, in both Jewish and Muslim traditions. Yet Hamas's leaders repeat that 'resistance is not an end in itself', hinting that they would be ready to adopt a purely political strategy when the time was right. Al-Qaeda's means include armed struggle in all its forms. It engages in conventional confrontation against combatants, but also conducts suicide bombings, targeting civilians without reservations.

Hamas limits its fight to within the borders of Palestine, and its enemy is Israel. Al-Qaeda considers the entire world to be its battlefield, and although its principal enemy is the United States the list of its enemies is open-ended. It includes those European countries that took part in the wars against Afghanistan and Iraq in 2002 and 2003, such as Italy, Spain and Poland. It also includes Muslim countries that are seen as western bases, such as Saudi Arabia, Pakistan and Morocco.

Hamas has never targeted westerners either inside or outside Palestine. This is a strict policy by the movement that has been adhered to over years without a single exception. Al-Qaeda, by contrast, considers westerners as legitimate targets anywhere, be they combatants or civilians. Attacking the World Trade Center on 9/11 was the culmination of al-Qaeda thinking and practice, and demonstrates the extent to which al-Qaeda will go in implementing its indiscriminate strategy. The similar atrocities committed by al-Qaeda against civilians by bombing trains in Madrid and London in March 2004 and July 2005 fall far outside any thinking or strategy of Hamas. So would the targeting of any other civilian groups of westerners, such as blowing up tourists, hotels or residential complexes of Western expats.

The nature of Hamas is also completely different from al-Qaeda. Hamas is a multifaceted social and political organization thriving within defined borders and parameters. The military provision of the movement is just one of its many other aspects. It is engaged in a political and democratic process like any other party, publicly and with very well-known leaders. Al-Qaeda, by contrast, is a completely secretive and underground organization. It almost confines itself to military activities without any political or social programmes. Democratic practices and peaceful means are ruled out completely.

Are we witnessing the rise of an 'Islamic and radical arc', starting from Iran, spanning Syria, Hizbullah and then Hamas?

When Hamas won the elections of 2006, Iran was on the rise, defying the United States and the world by enriching uranium, threatening to make the life and tasks of the American troops in Iraq very difficult, and supporting Syria and Hizbullah in Lebanon against US policies and allies. Iran was jubilant over Hamas's victory, and it started to talk about an 'arc of defiance' starting from Tehran, passing through Iraq where many of Iran's allies are, through Damascus to Lebanon's Hizbullah, and ending in Palestine with Hamas. This defiant alliance was meant to be against the United States and Israel and their arrogant policies in the region. In reality Iran's challenge to US policies in the region is tailored specifically to the US impasse in Iraq. While the vast majority of the Iraqi population and political and military groups would give loyalty to Iran in any confrontation with the United States, the Iranians temporarily enjoy a measure of leverage over the situation. Thousands of US soldiers in Iraq could be at the mercy of an Iranian decision to act one way or another.

Yet if the United States freed itself from the Iraqi dilemma, the situation could change and the regional influence of Iran could be circumvented. In all cases, Hamas would benefit from this 'arc of defiance' at least by strengthening its position and control of power for the next few years. One of the worst-case scenarios for almost all parties involved would be for Israel to attack Iran to prevent its development of any nuclear capacity. The repercussions of such a step are simply unimaginable.

8 Hamas and the West

HAMAS AND THE WEST

Does Hamas see the West as the enemy?

In general, Hamas's perception of the West is somewhat inimical. In common with prevailing thinking in Palestinian and Arab circles, Hamas holds the West – and particularly Britain, in the way that it handled both Zionist immigration in its Mandate-period administration and its pull-out in 1948 – responsible for the creation of Israel. This creation of a historically remote Jewish 'homeland' in 1948, in the heart of land that was and had been a solidly Arabic homeland for long centuries, resulted in endless troubles and an intractable bloody conflict. Hamas also blames the West, particularly the United States at the present, for continuous and unconditional support for Israel, at the complete expense of the Palestinian people, who are the only ones who seemingly have no rights in this matter. The West is perceived by Hamas, and by Palestinians in general, to be the staunch backer and protector of Israel.

Over the decades since 1948 western policies concerning the conflict in the Middle East have contributed to the cumulatively repulsive perceptions of the West held across the entire Arab world. Because of western support, Israel has acquired the mightiest military power in the region, including nuclear capabilities, from technology that was transferred to it in the first place by France and Britain, then by the United States. With western backing and a population of 6 million, Israel has also enjoyed a vibrant economy, with a 2005 GDP of US$121 billion. That is very close to the total of US$120 billion for the neighbouring Arab countries including Egypt, Syria and Jordan, whose total population is more than 105 million. Israel had a GDP per capita exceeding US$22,000, compared with a mere US$1,100 in the Palestinian case.

Other wars in the area were seen to have been encouraged or led by the West to further weaken the Arabs in the region and maintain a superior position for Israel. The two Gulf wars against Iraq in 1990 and in 2003 reinforced the thinking of Hamas, and many Palestinians and Arabs, that the West is and has been stridently against any Arab military power that could ever potentially counter Israel's military arsenal. Hamas has also repeatedly pointed out the influence that Jewish lobbies have had on the policies of western governments, particularly in the United States.

On the Palestinian issue specifically, Hamas sees the western countries as never having exerted any serious pressure on Israel to comply even with the long list of UN resolutions on Palestine drafted carefully by the West itself. This list starts with Resolution 191 of 1949, giving Palestinian refugees the right to return to their lands and compensation for losing their homes and properties, and for being forced out of Palestine by the creation of the State of Israel in 1948. Other UN resolutions were made in the aftermath of the 1967 war. After Israel's occupation of the West Bank (including East Jerusalem) and the Gaza Strip, the United Nations issued Resolutions 242 and 338 calling upon Israel to withdraw from 'lands that it occupied' and rejecting the Israeli annexation of East Jerusalem.

The Palestinians and Arabs in general have felt dismayed by almost every single UN resolution on Palestine. These resolutions have been drawn up, as Hamas has often reiterated, by the western powers in ways that have always ultimately secured the interests of Israel in the first place. However, Arabs and

Palestinians eventually accepted all these resolutions. The irony is that Western countries have shown a complete lack of commitment to the UN resolutions that they themselves have brokered, and no interest whatsoever in pressurizing their prodigy Israel to implement these resolutions.

Thus, what shapes Hamas's negative perception of the West is not only the legacy of past biased Western policies concerning the Palestine/Israel question, but also the current persistence in not changing these policies and doing nothing when agreed-upon solutions are not upheld. Even despite this Hamas does not consider the West to be its enemy. In its literature and declarations Hamas keeps confirming that its sole enemy is Israel, and its battlefield is clearly limited to the boundaries of the historic land of Palestine. This has been a pragmatic position by which Hamas has avoided expanding the line of combat with its foes. Over years of acquired experience and maturation, Hamas's view of the West has become more sophisticated, and it is able to differentiate between various players and their different policies.

Has Hamas targeted westerners inside or outside Palestine?

Hamas has never targeted Westerners either inside or outside Palestine. It has never considered individual westerners, or even western military and economic entities, as enemies or legitimate targets. The documented literature of Hamas as well as the record of events since its foundation attest not only to this strict policy but also to the ability of Hamas to uphold it. This policy is grounded firmly on two premises. The first premise relates to the above idea that Hamas does not consider the West either officially nor practically to be an enemy. Therefore, westerners and western institutions and interests in Israel or in the West Bank and the Gaza Strip have scrupulously never been targeted.

The second premise is that Hamas distinguishes clearly

between western policies and western individuals. It publicly and disparagingly criticises the West's biased policies over the conflict with Israel. Yet it has developed amicable contacts with many western organizations, experts, supporters and ordinary people. Hamas's leaders talk about people in the West as being kept in the dark over what their governments truly do against the people of the Middle East. They say that open-minded westerners who are keen to know about the situation in Palestine without prejudice easily understand the justness and fairness of the Palestinians' complaints.

Hamas's ascent to power in 2006 has only enhanced its pragmatic policies towards the West and westerners. Senior officials, leaders of the movement and ministers of Hamas's government have all shown eagerness to open channels with the West. Despite the initial US-EU embargo against Hamas, its government has managed to defiantly survive that and to increasingly broaden its network of contacts with western officials and institutions.

What are Hamas's perceptions of western civilization and ideals?

Hamas's views on western civilisation and its ideals have basically been drawn from the somewhat entrenched school of thought of its mother movement, the Muslim Brotherhood. Its view is based on demarcating theoretical distinctions between the scientific, technological and administrative aspects of western civilisation, and its underlying philosophies and values. Hamas, as well as other mainstream Islamist movements, accepts what it sees to be the 'neutral scientific' advancements of the West, and faces no principled trouble in borrowing and using them. It refuses to countenance, however, what it considers to be the 'materialistic morality' of Western modernity, and the lack of spirituality: the marginalization of the divine, and the secularization of humanity.

In practice, Hamas's dealing with, and *de facto* adoption of, 'imports' of western political modernity expose the relative infirmity of the theoretical distinction between these technological and non-technological aspects of the West. In the absence of sufficient Hamas literature on these issues specifically, Hamas's political practice shows that the movement is actually absorbing more 'western' values than it would like to acknowledge. Aspects of western-sourced political modernity have been consciously or subconsciously internalized by Hamas and manifested in its political, organizational and societal interactions. For example, the very nature of Hamas's liberation struggle has evolved on the nation-state concept (not the borderless Islamic *Ummah* notion), its party-based hierarchy follows the formation of political parties in the West, its internal affairs are run on western democratic practices, and its political rhetoric encompasses such western notions as human rights and citizenship, in addition to the rule of the majority and the rule of law.

Many of Hamas's senior figures, and since 2006 Hamas's cabinet ministers, were trained in the West, or at universities that teach according to western methods. Hamas's experts in various fields such as science, agriculture, administration, accounting, urban and rural planning, education, medicine and engineering perform their expertise in ways that were originally western-fashioned. As can be seen with many other blue-collar Islamists, underneath the religious wrappings and appearances lies a technocrat essence that is driven by the pursuit of perfection and self-interest.

HAMAS AND THE UNITED STATES

What perceptions do the United States and Hamas have of each other?

The US perception of Hamas almost reproduces the Israeli one. When Hamas first emerged in the late 1980s and early

1990s, there were signs of tentative, pragmatic soundings. Indirect contacts and messages were delivered to Hamas via US ambassadors in the region, or people around them. The stated aim was to closely 'explore' the positions and attitudes of the rising movement. In late 1992 and early 1993 the Americans had official contact and meetings with senior Hamas members in Amman, through the US embassy there. In those years, Israel itself was still hoping that the growing power of Hamas would eventually undermine the PLO and its main Fatah movement. Thus the low-key US 'exploring' course of action was indirectly approved of by Israel, insomuch as Israel hoped that the United States would influence Hamas to change its views and strategies.

But as the US/Hamas contacts themselves caught public attention Israel protested, and the US side abruptly ended them. Hamas denounced the US decision to cut off contact, saying that it clearly proved the deep-rooted influence of the Jewish lobby on Washington. Thereafter, the official US position hardened quickly against Hamas. Weeks after ending contact with Hamas, Washington labelled the movement 'a terrorist organization' in its April 1993 report on global terrorism. Initial discussions on whether Hamas was a liberation movement or a terrorist organization were prematurely suppressed within circles of policymakers in Washington.

Later on, and following Hamas's embracing of the strategy of suicide bombings on a large scale in 1995 and 1996, the official US position grew more hostile. Washington exerted enormous pressure on the Fatah-led Palestinian Authority during that time to suppress Hamas and dismantle its armed wing, a demand that always fell beyond the Palestinian Authority's capacity. Back home, US authorities banned the work of several Islamic and Palestinian associations and charities in the United States because they were accused of sponsoring Hamas. Politically, the Americans threw their weight with the Palestinian Authority, and saw no role for Hamas unless it would disarm itself completely, denounce 'terrorism' and recognize Israel. Hamas was not interested.

Over the next few years, in addition to their direct and bilateral assault, the United States and Israel continued to lobby the European Union to also proscribe Hamas. The European Union partly yielded and officially decided to consider the military wing of Hamas as a terrorist organization (see more below). The United States declared its 'war on terror' in the aftermath of the 9/11 al-Qaeda attacks in New York and Washington in 2001, and Hamas was further targeted. Pro-Israel neoconservatives in Washington lumped Hamas in with organizations such as al-Qaeda. In doing so they fulfilled Israeli demands to neutralize the 'national liberation dimension' of Hamas, and relegate it to simply being part of 'global terror', although the differences between Hamas and al-Qaeda are many and unmistakable (see Chapter 7).

Washington faced the most difficult test concerning Hamas when the movement emerged victorious in the Palestinian Legislative Council (PLC) elections in January 2006. Hamas legitimately formed a government which was promptly attacked by the United States for neither recognizing Israel nor abandoning 'violence'. Ironically, these Palestinian elections themselves had been part of overdue democratic reforms that the Palestinian Authority had been pressured by the Americans and Europeans to undertake. The democracy that the United States had advocated in Palestine as well as in other Arab countries in the period preceding the elections had indeed brought Hamas to power. However, when it came down to it, the United States rejected the outcome of Palestinian democracy and mobilized an international political and financial embargo against the newly formed government. Succeeding in persuading the European Union to join forces with it, it stopped all financial aid to the Palestinians, bringing millions of Palestinians who mostly rely on the salaries paid by the Palestinian Authority to the verge of starvation.

On the other hand, the Hamas perception of the United States has also developed radically in response to the US 'unilateral war' on Hamas. It has just managed to stop one step short from considering the United States an enemy. The theoretical under-pinnings upon which Hamas forms its relations with the world, and with western countries in particular, have remained intact, however. These stress that 'Hamas's dealings with foreign states and international organizations, regardless of any pre-existing political and ideological baggage, will serve the interests of the Palestinian people, their cause, and their rights.' The movement has managed to hold its official line on not attacking other states: 'Hamas has no dispute with any foreign state or international organization, and the movement's policy is not to attack the interests or possessions of foreign states.'

Hamas's government has followed the same line of policy and kept all channels and possibilities open for a new chapter, as a democratically elected Palestinian government dealing with the United States. The latter has shown no interest.

HAMAS AND EUROPE

What perceptions do Europe and Hamas have of each other?

In common with other Palestinian and Arab views, Hamas has nurtured a slightly friendlier attitude to contemporary Europe than to the United States. Europe also used to adopt a different line of policies about the Arab/Israeli conflict in general and the legitimacy of Palestinian rights than the United States.

Hamas looks at Europe as a diverse pool of powers. What separates individual European countries on major foreign issues, demonstrated in the lack of an effective common EU foreign policy, transcends what unites them. Thus, British, French, Spanish and Italian positions on Palestine and Hamas vary. These policies even differ from, for example, one Scandi-navian country to another, Norway being a prime example of just one odd man out. Given this, Hamas has kept channels open and always pursued new ones with Europe. Both on the collective EU level and on the individual state level, Hamas has managed to have its voice heard in a reasonable way. Through European embassies in the Middle East, or through diplomats in the West Bank and the Gaza Strip, Hamas has maintained quiet European contacts.

Yet in September 2003 the European Union decided to denounce Hamas, while joining the US 'war on terror'. This decision implied that Hamas members, leaders or affiliated organizations would be banned from operating in any EU countries – something that never actually took place anyway. But to the dismay of Hamas and many European experts and diplomats, this pronouncement on the part of the European Union could only be viewed as European collusion with hostile US foreign policy as pursued by the neoconservatives. With that decision the European Union has effectively crippled itself from playing an effective role in Hamas-related Palestinian affairs. In particular, the European Union has jeopardized its pivotal role in brokering temporary 'truces' with Hamas, which it played several times during the second *intifada* of 2000.

The European Union has also been perplexed on other issues concerning Hamas. A major one is how to deal with the effective and widespread grassroots Hamas-affiliated organizations. On the ground, and apart from the aid directed to the PA government, multi millions of annual EU funds have to be channelled to NGOs for community projects, where the social-charitable bedrock of Hamas has been very efficient. It would be strongly questionable to fund only ineffectual and often corrupt non-Hamas-run organizations, while dismissing effective and transparent Hamas ones. This dilemma multiplied even more when Hamas won the majority of local municipality elections in 2005 in the West Bank and Gaza Strip. Municipalities are the main providers of basic living services, and have always been thought of as apolitical bodies that the European Union could deal with financially without sensitivities. When the social-charitable wing of Hamas took control of most of them, and in a short period of time showed considerable achievements, the European Union was further embarrassed by not cooperating with them.

Since Hamas formed its government as a result of winning the 2006 PLC elections, the European Union has faced the same dilemma but on an unprecedented scale. Hamas is now the official democratically elected government of the Palestinians, the address at which the European Union should be dealing. Unlike the United States, the European Union is looked on by the majority of Palestinians as more even-handed, humane and sensitive towards the suffering of the Palestinians, and less under the yoke of Jewish-Israeli lobbying. Thus, Europe has been shouldering a moral burden that materializes in the form of humanitarian assistance to the Palestinians, a burden which, it has to be said, has also been approved and acknowledged by other players, including the United States itself.

The European dilemma over Hamas was compounded exponentially in the April 2006 decision to suspend all forms of official aid to the Palestinians, pending Hamas's recognition of Israel and denunciation of violence. EU foreign ministers have approved a temporary suspension of US$600 million in annual aid to the Palestinians. Ben Bot, the Dutch foreign minister, voiced the justification of this move when he said, 'The Palestinian people have opted for this government, so they will have to bear the consequences.'

For its part, Hamas's government has resolutely refused conditional aid but has tried to tone down its militant discourse. It has strongly condemned the European decision, which it considers to be a collective punishment against the Palestinian people. The entire reaction against the Palestinian elections has been viewed by Hamas, and many others, as a scandalous exemplification of hypocritical western politics. An outcome of free and fair democratic elections has been shamefully rejected because the winners are not pro-West, or willing to accept or implement what has been imposed on them by their enemy, Israel. Hamas, however, has been able to do something of what it does best – exploiting the cracks and differences, in this case between European countries – to make some leaps over and around some of the obstacles of the EU decision. Again, quietly several European countries have acted outside the 'official EU policy', and are maintaining their channels and cooperation with the Hamas government.

Are we going to see Hamas members as Palestinian ambassadors in London, Paris, Brussels, and Washington, among other capitals?

It is not a remote possibility that senior Hamas members will be acting as Palestinian ambassadors in Western and European cities. The far more highly unlikely idea of Hamas having become the Palestinian government in the first place has already materialized. If Hamas survives the enormous pressures inside Palestine and the international blockade imposed on its government, all possibilities are open. In principle, the Hamas-run Palestinian foreign ministry has the discretion of appointing Palestinian ambassadors around the world. Judging from Hamas's past eagerness to cultivate its image and public relations, it should be expected that Hamas will reshuffle the current Palestinian diplomatic structure. Perhaps there are two reasons that will induce Hamas to do so. First will be the urgent need to reform Palestinian foreign affairs, in terms of both organization and message. Many of the present long-serving Palestinian ambassadors have run out of ideas and enthusiasm, especially those who have spent long head-banging years in their current posts – up to 20 years in certain cases. Equally important to Hamas will be the need to dispatch envoys abroad who are orga-nizationally closer to the movement, or loyal to its political line. But once again, all depends on how successful Hamas's govern-ment will be in enduring the initial siege that it is facing in these early days.

9 Hamas's leadership and structure

LEADERSHIP

What does the leadership hierarchy of Hamas look like?

The leadership structure of Hamas is divided into two somewhat parallel but slightly dissimilar parts, one inside Palestine and one outside Palestine. The 'inside' leadership has always been promoted from the rank and file of the movement via internal elections, a practice that is well established within Islamist movements that have a Muslim Brotherhood background and traditions. The 'outside' leadership evolved differently because Hamas understandably does not have the same sort of membership organization outside Palestine that is has in the West Bank and the Gaza Strip. This outside-Palestine leadership was originally formed in coordination with the 'inside' Hamas, primarily as a back-up mechanism at the time the movement was formed in the late 1980s. It was plausibly thought that Hamas would need external support, financially and politically, and this was to be the job of the outside leadership in exile.

The strictly disciplined membership of Hamas is drawn from across poor and middle-class Palestinians, with a strong presence in refugee camps and most deprived areas. Many better-off Palestinians too give their loyalty to Hamas, in cities that are well known to be traditionally conservative such as Hebron. Members of Hamas in local areas elect their representatives to the leading party body, *Majlis ash-Shoura* (the Consultative Council) which is charged with outlining the overall strategy of the Hamas movement. This council in turn chooses members of the smaller 'Political Bureau' of between 10 and 20 people, who deal with daily affairs. The Consultative Council and the Political Bureau establish specialized committees that look after various aspects of Hamas's activities: charitable and social, educational, membership, military, financial, media and public relations, religious, women's and so on. There is considerable, if deliberate, vagueness on the exact chain of 'command and control' between the top political leadership and the military wing Izzedin al-Qassam. For security reasons, Hamas keeps ample distance between the functioning of each of its branches, and distances all of them from the military wing in particular.

Hamas's leadership is effectively divided between three geographical areas: the West Bank, the Gaza Strip (both inside Palestine) and exile communities, largely in Jordan, Lebanon and Syria (constituting 'outside' Palestine). It is a matter of judgement which of the three enjoys more power. The opinion that the Hamas branch and leadership in the Gaza Strip is the most powerful has strong grounds. In general, the balance of power has always favoured the inside leadership. After Hamas came to power in 2006, the inside leadership was strengthened even further. But while it is safe to say that the two-branched inside leadership (in the West Bank and the Gaza Strip) controls the muscles of the movement, the outside leadership controls financial resources and external contacts.

Over the years, this three-branched leadership has managed to exhibit an astonishing 'decision-making management'. The challenge Hamas has faced in this regard has included not only shared decision making, but also day-to-day procedural management and coordination between the three branches. Hamas's spokespeople keep emphasizing the 'collective leadership' nature of their movement over personalities, and in practice they have shown a significant amount of adherence to this principle. As yet, there have been no authoritarian personalities or ultra-charismatic leaders who have used their influence to impose any individual vision on the entire movement, such as was the case with the PLO, Fatah and Yasser Arafat, for example.

How cohesive and united is Hamas, and are there radicals and moderates inside it?

Hamas is a highly sophisticated organization, with a coherent structure and strong culture of internal solidarity. It is the only Palestinian organization that has preserved its unity and integrity over the almost six decades of struggle against colonial Zionism. Since its formation there have been no splits or even small splinter groups breaking away. This is partly due to the religious values that encourage cohesion and disparage rifts, and partly due to its organizational background, which is rooted in the Muslim Brotherhood culture where members prioritize unity over contested views. Also, the challenges that have faced Hamas have fed into its united stand. Confronted by extreme Israeli measures since it was established, and then by a series of crackdowns by the Fatah-led Palestinian Authority since 1994, a sense of solidarity and purpose has only been consolidated further by all these security limitations and even arrests in neighbouring Arab countries.

Although Hamas has remained cohesive, the movement has witnessed the emergence of various and different views on some of the major issues. Moderate and radical voices have been markedly present at certain conjunctures, especially regarding the continuation of the strategy of suicide attacks. Some senior figures would project staunch positions on one issue, where others would use milder tones, leaving the door ajar for options and interpretations. The most important observation, however, is that there has been no development of any discrete group within Hamas that is geographically based, or politically or ideologically cohesive, that could be labelled as a 'radical' or 'moderate' faction. It is particularly inaccurate to issue a general description of the 'outside' or 'inside' leadership of Hamas as either moderate or radical, or to say that Hamas in the Gaza Strip is more radical than Hamas in the West Bank, or vice versa. Actually, moderate and radical voices do exist within all three existing branches of the movement.

Therefore, the dichotomy of radicals/moderates that some people try to apply to the outside/inside leaderships of Hamas, or to the Gaza Strip/West Bank Hamas, is somewhat pointless. One of the reasons that Hamas has remained united is the inapplicability of that dichotomy to any geographical/ideological separation between its three branches. Had the moderate voices, or the radicals for that matter, overwhelmingly existed in any one of those areas, Hamas would have faced serious trouble and could have split up.

The cohesion and unity of Hamas has, however, faced the most serious challenge since its foundation after it assumed power in the elections of January 2006. Hamas has had to harmonize its organizational responsibilities with governmental ones under tremendous Israeli and western pressure, without losing the confidence of the people and with close coordination between its three branches. The challenge is extremely complex: top Hamas leaders inside or outside Palestine versus the Hamas prime minister, Hamas government ministers versus Hamas movement leaders, Hamas's external relationships versus the foreign affairs of the Hamas government, and so on. Power and responsibility will inevitably be fragmented, disputed and fought over, and keeping all that under control has required and will require extraordinary skills. Only time will tell if the united Hamas that existed before winning the elections will remain the same now it is in power.

What is the relationship between the political and military wings of Hamas?

The political leadership is the ultimate authority in Hamas. All other wings and branches are subject to the strategy and guidelines that are drawn by Hamas's Consultative Council and Political Bureau (PB). As mentioned earlier Hamas is multi-functional, and has separate 'agencies' to deliver its overall services and strategy. In relation to Hamas's military action it is the political leadership that decides whether at a certain period of time the military wing should carry on, halt military operations, increase or reduce them. Thus, the giving of a general green or red light is calculated politically and channelled through to the military.

At the same time, however, members of the political leadership repeatedly, and in all likelihood truthfully, claim that they know nothing about the specific operational technicalities of the military wing. For security reasons, Hamas's political leadership is kept almost in complete darkness about any detailed timing and places of attacks beforehand. So while the military wing functions virtually independently, executionally speaking, it is governed by a political strategy that is drawn and exercised by the political leadership.

A central question in this context is, if Hamas were to declare a ceasefire, is its military wing disciplined enough to implement it? Drawing on past experience the immediate answer is 'Most likely, yes.' But matters have become more complicated since Hamas has gained control of the Palestinian Authority, where the stakes are now higher, and expectations more weighty. More room has opened up for dissatisfaction and friction between the political and military wings. Previously, the military wing of Hamas has shown a great deal of discipline. On several occasions when Hamas's political leadership decided to stop military attacks for either political, security or strategic considerations, the military wing acted accordingly. In the lifetime of the organization there has been no rift visible between the two Hamas wings.

However, a major shift has taken place since Hamas became

the Palestinian Authority, which was the administration that
Hamas used to criticize and ignore when carrying out military
attacks against the will and plans of that authority. Having said
that, for at least a year prior to its assumption of power Hamas
committed itself to 'a period of calm' brokered by Egypt, according to which Israel would stop targeting Hamas leaders and
Hamas would stop its attacks. After Hamas's victory it extended
(unilaterally) that period of calm. Hamas acknowledged the pressure of other priorities which needed to be addressed urgently by
the now Hamas government, and set aside the headache of
military attacks at least until matters became clearer.

As Hamas has halted its attacks against Israel during its self-
proclaimed period of calm, Fatah and other Palestinian factions
have started their own series of attacks, partly to embarrass
Hamas and partly in response to the unstoppable Israeli attacks
which are also aimed at provoking Hamas. While neither retaliating against the Israeli provocations, nor matching the attacks of
rival factions, Hamas's military wing has started showing signs of
dissatisfaction and unrest. At the time of writing there has been no
visible rift, but events are developing quickly and leave all
possibilities open.

Hamas's worst-case scenario in this context is that its political leadership loses control over its military, or part of it. It is not
unlikely that angry groups within the Izzedin al-Qassam military
brigades of Hamas could split up into more radical and discon-
nected cells. This would be a really bleak scenario not only for
Hamas but for the Palestinian situation as a whole. It could create
an Algerian-like condition where the biggest Islamist movement
splintered into unfocused extreme groups.

*Who is Sheikh Ahmad Yasin, the founder of Hamas, and
what is his significance?*

Sheikh Ahmad Yasin is considered to be the founder, the spiritual figurehead and the most historic figure of Hamas. Fully

paralyzed in a wheelchair since he was eleven years old, the calm and charismatic leader was until his death the most popular personality in the Gaza Strip. At the age of 66 he was killed by an Israeli helicopter, along with nine other Palestinians, just after finishing dawn prayers on 22 March 2004 at one of the Gaza City mosques.

When Yasin was aged ten, in 1948, his family and tens of thousands of Palestinians were forced out of their homes and villages and driven to areas outside the 'redistributed' territory that would ever since be known as Israel. He and his family became 'refugees' in the Gaza Strip, where he lived a miserable and illness-plagued life. Despite his bad health he became very active politically and religiously. Sheikh Yasin was one of the founders of the Muslim Brotherhood in the Gaza Strip, as well as the founder of the 'Islamic Complex', an Islamic educational and charitable institution that was for many years the centre of Islamic activism in the area.

A schoolteacher by profession Sheikh Yasin ('sheikh', in addition to being a formal title of address for a hereditary chieftain or village leader, is often and in this case used by the community simply as a mark of deep affection and respect) was sentenced to prison twice by the Israeli military courts, first for 13 years in 1985, then for life in 1991 on charges of directing military cells against Israeli soldiers. On both occasions he was eventually freed through deals. In 1985 Israel was compelled to free him with other Palestinian prisoners in return for releasing Israeli soldiers captured by Palestinian factions in South Lebanon. In 1997 he was freed after pressure by the late King Hussein of Jordan, who became infuriated with Israel for sending spies to Jordan to try to assassinate another Hamas leader, Khaled Mish'al, who was in the country at that time.

Sheikh Yasin was Hamas's main ideologue, mobilizer, pragmatist and populist. Projecting the typical model of a restless Islamist leader whose pragmatism never eclipsed his dreams of a principled utopia, Yasin's views and perceptions have formed to a large extent the political orientation of the movement. It was he who suggested the idea of *hudna* (truce), with which Hamas could reach a mutual ceasefire with Israel without breaking from its religious or nationalist principles. It was he who declared that 'civil war' between Palestinians was a 'no go' area. Even if Hamas was continuously attacked by the Palestinian Authority and its main Fatah faction, Hamas should never retaliate, Yasin insisted, because that could lead to internecine Palestinian war. At the social and religious level, Yasin accumulated rare authority in the Gaza Strip. He was a respected arbitrator and judge to whom families and parties in dispute could go and settle their differences.

Yasin's influence preserved a great sense of unity inside Hamas, for he functioned above the level of competition among the second-ranking leaders. But the very same unassailable position of respect indirectly crippled the emergence of innovative ideas and initiatives that could have been suggested by others. Other figures felt the need to stay close to Yasin's ideas so that they were not alienated by the wider membership because of their views. Even after his death, Yasin's legacy and statements are repeatedly referred to by current leaders and senior figures of Hamas.

Another aspect that deserves attention in this context is the simplicity and modesty of Hamas's leaders and its senior personalities. These virtues have always amassed great popularity to Hamas. The highest-ranking Hamas leaders still live side by side with poor and ordinary people. Sheikh Ahmad Yasin, the founder of Hamas, lived and eventually was killed in the very same refugee camp to which his family had been forcibly resettled when he was a child in 1948.

Even the prime minister of Hamas's government, Ismail Haniya, refused to leave his modest lower-class house and move to the comfortable residence of the former prime minister. In the first cabinet meeting of Hamas's government, which lasted for six hours on 5 April 2006, Haniya and his ministers had very simple *humous* and *falafel* sandwiches bought from the local shop for their lunch.

The cabinet declared that it would reduce by half all the salaries of the ministers and members of parliament, and would never pay them until all other Palestinians had received their salaries. The speaker of the parliament, Aziz Duwaik, another Hamas personality, refused to be allocated a special car with security and protection. He said that he 'will never cost the government budget an extra penny'. Likewise, members of Hamas's leadership outside Palestine project a modest style of life and conduct. For example, Khaled Mish'al, head of Hamas's Political Bureau, surprised other passengers in economy class during his trip from Riyadh to Damascus in March 2006. The Palestinian people compare this simple and close-to-the-people behaviour with the lavish lifestyle and arrogance of top leaders of the defeated Fatah movement and previous senior members of the Palestinian Authority.

Who are the most powerful leaders of Hamas?

Throughout Hamas's lifetime a number of names and faces have become familiar to the outside world as the main figures and spokespeople for the movement. In addition to Sheikh Ahmad Yasin, mentioned above, below is a list of people whose influence and roles are central in the formation of Hamas and its current politics. Yet before discussing these individuals it is helpful to say that Hamas leaders (especially those who are inside Palestine) project an almost common profile. The vast majority have come from poor refugee camps or the lower middle class; gained university education; belonged in their early youth to the Muslim Brotherhood organization either in the West Bank or the Gaza Strip (or abroad in the case of the outside leadership); spent a number of years in Israeli prisons; and either have been killed or have been targeted to be killed by the Israeli army. In terms of religious adherence, all of Hamas's leaders are deeply religious and conservative by the standards of ordinary Muslims. Their observance of Islamic teachings at the individual, family and societal level is visible, and it is a fundamental aspect of their personalities. The selective list below includes leaders from all three geographical branches where Hamas leadership operates: the West Bank, the Gaza Strip and in exile.

Abdul Aziz al-Rantisi (Gaza Branch, assassinated by Israel)

For many years al-Rantisi was considered to be the second in the leadership ranking after Sheikh Ahmad Yasin, the movement's long-time and spiritual leader. Al-Rantisi assumed leadership of Hamas in the Gaza Strip in spring 2004 after the Israelis assassinated Sheikh Yasin. Less than a month after that, however, al-Rantisi himself was assassinated. He was one of the founders of Hamas and a lifelong comrade of Sheikh Yasin. Charismatic and articulate by nature, he combined modesty towards his 'brothers' in the movement and toughness towards his enemies, which made him widely popular within Hamas and with Palestinians at large. He held hardline views but never contradicted Yasin's more moderate outlook. Secular Palestinian politicians and intellectuals were never impressed by his politics or discourse, however. He was perceived by them to be a master at packaging unrealistic demands in very powerful religious rhetoric.

Al-Rantisi was born in 1947 in a village near Jaffa. A year after that, in the wake of the British pull-out from Palestine, war broke out between Zionist and Arab factions, and with the imposition of the new state of Israel hundreds of thousands of Palestinians were driven from their villages and cities, including al-Rantisi's family, who ended up in the Khan Yunis refugee camp in the Gaza area. He went up through high school there, travelled to Egypt to study medicine, then returned to Khan Yunis as a paediatric practitioner. In later stages, he became a lecturer at the Islamic University of Gaza.

From his early youth he was politically active with a clear-cut Islamic leaning, and a member of the Palestinian Muslim Brotherhood organization. After the founding of Hamas, he was arrested several times, then in 1992 deported to South Lebanon for one year with more than 400 Palestinians. He was immediately jailed upon his return in 1993, and remained in jail until 1997. A year after his release, he was jailed again but this time by the Palestinian Authority (yielding to Israeli pressure) because of his Hamas activities. When the jail itself was targeted by Israeli shelling, the Palestinian Authority released him and other Palestinians. In June 2003 he narrowly escaped an Israeli attempt to assassinate him, during which his body guard and a child passer-by were killed. His successful assassination a year later gave way to the rise of Mahmoud al-Zahhar.

Mahmoud al-Zahhar (Gaza Branch, foreign minister in the Hamas government)

Born in 1945, al-Zahhar is a veteran Hamas figure who became the foreign minister in Hamas's elected government in early 2006. He studied medicine in Cairo, where he obtained a master's degree, then practised as a doctor in the Gaza Strip. During his early youth, first in Gaza then in Egypt, al-Zahhar became an active member of the Muslim Brotherhood. He was the founder of several medical societies and co-founder of the Islamic University in Gaza.

He has been known for a long time as one of Hamas's relatively moderate voices. At one point in 1996 he issued a rare independent public appeal through the media to Hamas's military wing Izzedin al-Qassam, asking them to halt their suicide attacks. Immediately, he was harshly criticized by members of Hamas and temporarily marginalized.

After the assassination of Sheikh Yasin and al-Rantisi he was elected as Hamas's leader in the Gaza Strip. He himself was the target of several assassination attempts by the Israelis. In September 2003 an Israeli F16 bombed his house in Gaza, wounding him and his daughter and killing his 29-year-old son Khaled. The house was destroyed and many other people were killed or wounded. The impact of that attack and the great loss of his son, combined with an increasing drive on his part to compensate for his lack of the charisma that his two predecessors enjoyed, led to Al-Zahhar's stance and discourse becoming noticeably radicalized compared with his initial leanings. Yet when he became foreign minister he issued mixed messages of moderation and radicalism, and the more moderate Zahhar started to take over once again.

Early on, al-Zahhar was perhaps the first of Hamas's figures to talk about a 'pragmatic' interim solution to the conflict with Israel. In March 1988, four months after the foundation of Hamas, he presented a four-point proposal to Shimon Peres, then the Israeli foreign minister, which included the following:

1   Israel would declare its willingness to withdraw from the territories it occupied in 1967, including Jerusalem in particular.
2   The Occupied Territories would be placed in the custody of the United Nations.
3   The Palestinian people inside and outside Palestine would name their representatives to the peace talks in whatever manner they chose. Israel could not object to the choice unless the Palestinians also had the right to object to the representatives of Israel.
4   At a time agreed by both sides, negotiations would begin among the representatives concerning all issues relating to all rights.

Ismail Haniya (Gaza Branch, prime minister in the Hamas government)

Born in the Shati refugee camp in Gaza, Haniya has grown up completely immersed in the misery of the Palestinians who lost their land and ended up in impoverished refugee camps. His family was displaced from Asqalan near Jaffa during the 1948 war. Haniya finished his university degree in Arabic language studies from the Islamic University in Gaza, where his leadership fortunes were shaped as a prominent figure among the Islamist students in the early 1980s.

With the formation of Hamas, Haniya was at the forefront as one of the youngest founding members. After the first *intifada* in 1987 he was arrested several times, and in 1992 he was deported to South Lebanon with more than 400 Islamist activists. Although Haniya was less visible to the outside world than the two above-mentioned senior members, he was no less significant. A well-known moderate voice within Hamas, Haniya amassed deep respect with the membership and great popularity within the broader Palestinian constituency. Sheikh Yasin, the spiritual leader of Hamas, appointed him as his first confidant and aide, and he remained close to Yasin until the latter's death.

Haniya is one of the most acknowledged moderate senior figures in Hamas. He was always the man who sought settlements between his group and its foes. During periods of friction between Hamas and other Palestinian factions, Haniya has always been seen as a moderator who is trusted by all parties and able to pacify volatile situations. His calmness and popularity, modesty and moderation led Hamas to charge him with the responsibility of leading its 2006 election campaign, which it won roundly.

Hamas decided to boycott the 1996 elections for the first Palestinian Legislative Council – which was set up according to the Oslo Agreements signed two years earlier between Israel and the PLO – because 'they were an outcome of the capitulating Oslo deal'. Haniya and three other Hamas figures decided to run for the elections, in opposition to the movement's stand. Under mounting pressure, Haniya and his colleagues backed down and adhered to the Hamas official line. At the time,

Haniya explained his pro-participation position to this author, which gives great glimpses into his political thinking. He outlined eight carefully written points that show the advantages of taking part in the elections, as follows:

- Participation in the elections will not amount to a surrender of Hamas's political position as long as the movement contests the elections under the banner of all the principles with which it is identified.
- Participation would guarantee a legitimate political presence for the movement after the elections, and Hamas would have secured a guarantee against decrees that could outlaw the movement.
- Hamas would be kept informed of, and be in a position to participate in, the formulation of legislation governing civil society that will emanate from the elected Council, thus securing a guarantee against exclusion.
- Hamas would be in a position to introduce significant and badly needed reforms in domestic institutions and could combat the spread of corruption.
- Hamas could participate in the creation of official institutions, something for which it always has asked, in keeping with its emphatic desire to participate in civil society and to promote internal development.
- Hamas would be well informed of developments in the final status negotiations and what is to come after that.
- Hamas would secure protection for itself and the institutions it has sponsored over the years, and its political leaders and prominent figures would enjoy parliamentary immunity.
- Participation in the elections would be a response to the demand of a significant number of our people who are looking for honest alternative and God-fearing candidates so that they can rest at ease about action in various areas of life.

Aziz Duwaik (West Bank Branch, speaker of the Palestinian Parliament)

Born in 1948 in Hebron, the West Bank, into a middle-class family, Duwaik completed his high school in the city, and then obtained three master's degrees in education and urban planning before he finished his PhD in urban planning at the University of Pennsylvania. In his early years he joined the Muslim Brotherhood then Hamas, and became a prominent personality in the city of Hebron. He was deported to South Lebanon in 1992 with other Hamas members for one year, where he became very well known as the English-speaking spokesman for the 415 deportees. After his return to Hebron he distanced himself from political activities, immersing himself in his academic professorship at al-Najah University, where he established the Department of Geography.

His almost sudden reappearance on the public scene after the election, when he was chosen by Hamas as the speaker of the Parliament, was surprising. Because little is known about his political qualities, some question whether he is really fit for the post. Others see his appointment as a smart move on the part of Hamas, who are bringing to such a high-ranking position a man with no enemies and a very well-known moderate and professional. Also, his appointment as effectively the third most powerful person in the Palestinian Authority hierarchy (after the president and the prime minister) has reflected Hamas's determination to maintain tight control on power. According to the Palestinian constitution, Duwaik would replace the president Abu Mazen should the latter become incapable of undertaking his responsibilities.

Naser al-Sha'er (West Bank Branch, deputy prime minister and minister of education and higher education)

Born in 1961 in Nablus in the West Bank, al-Sha'er is one of the new faces of Hamas who came to public notice at the formation of Hamas's government in 2006. He was an active member and leader of the Islamic bloc at al-Najah University in Nablus, before he left to study in the United Kingdom, where he finished his PhD in Middle East studies at Manchester University. Al-Sha'er has accumulated experience not only in political activism but also in the academic field and research. In the late 1990s he embarked on a course on religion and democracy at New York University as a research scholar. Before joining the Hamas government he served as the dean of Islamic Studies and Law at al-Najah University for five years.

Al-Sha'er is considered to be one of the moderate voices within Hamas. His training and travel in the West exposed him to the complexities of world politics and left a visible realist stamp on his thinking. From the Islamic perspective, he has written and published on various subjects such as human rights, the religious curriculum in Palestine, globalization, gender and familial violence. Unless he is sidelined by hardliners in the movement, al-Sha'er will be pivotal in shaping part of Hamas's thinking in the near future. By virtue of his strong background in Islamic studies combined with his modern understanding and sophistication, he could be in the position of theorizing new paths for Hamas in the short term.

Khaled Mish'al (Exile Branch, head of the Political Bureau)

Born in 1956 in the village of Silwad near Ramallah in the West Bank, Mish'al was displaced with his family to Kuwait after the war of 1967. He finished his studies in physics at the University of Kuwait, where he was an active leader of the Islamic bloc, which was the local manifestation of the Palestinian Muslim Brotherhood. In the late 1980s he became involved in the external leadership circles of the newly established Hamas.

Following the Iraqi invasion of Kuwait he and his family, along with thousands of previously displaced Palestinians, moved to Jordan where he started to become more known as a Hamas member and continued his Hamas external support. In

1996 Mish'al replaced Mousa Abu Marzouq as the top leader of Hamas outside Palestine, after the arrest of Marzouq in the United States. In Amman where Hamas's exile leadership was operating (only in the political and media areas as agreed with the Jordanian authorities), Mossad agents attempted to assassinate Mish'al in September 1997 but he survived.

In 1999 the relationship between Hamas and the Jordanian authorities soured greatly after the United States and Israel put pressure on the King of Jordan to expel Hamas's leadership, which he did in November of that year. Since then, the official address of Mish'al has been Damascus, although he moves constantly between more than one country in the region including Lebanon, Qatar and Iran.

Mish'al is the face of Hamas outside Palestine, charged with strengthening the movement's relationship with governments and outside organizations. In rallying support for Hamas among states and individuals both inside and outside Arab and Islamic circles, there are times when some stand at odds with the other; Mish'al conveys moderate and radical views concurrently, appeasing different audiences. Although articulate and popular among Hamas supporters and within Islamic circles, he is seen by others as lacking charisma and leadership sophistication.

Mousa Abu Marzouq (Exile Branch, deputy chief of Hamas's Political Bureau)

Born in 1951 in the Rafah refugee camp in Gaza, his family was originally displaced from Yebna village near Majdal during the 1948 war. After finishing his high school in the Gaza Strip he travelled to Cairo, where he obtained in 1976 a university degree in mechanical engineering, then moved to the United Arab Emirates for work. In 1981 he moved to the United States to continue postgraduate studies, and remained there until he finished his PhD in 1992.

Starting his Islamist political activism in high school then continuing in Egypt and the United Arab Emirates, his actual rise in prominence came among the Islamic societies in the United States where he headed several associations. By the time of the eruption of the first *intifada* in 1987, he had become very active in supporting and speaking for Hamas. Early on he helped in the establishment of the Islamic University in Gaza, and occupied a seat on its board of governors. Working behind the scenes he was free to travel between the Gaza Strip, Egypt, the Gulf and the United States, organizing the well-being of the newly established movement. In 1989 he reorganized the structure of Hamas after it had been badly affected by continuous Israeli crackdowns and arrests.

He moved from the United States to Jordan in 1992, when he was chosen as the head of Hamas's Political Bureau. His new position, however, did not deter him from visiting the United States several times for private business and political activism within Islamic organisations there supportive to Hamas. But he was arrested in 1995 in a New York airport, after Jordan's decision to expel him, and remained in a US jail until May 1997, when he was deported to Jordan. Hamas installed Khaled Mish'al in his place as head of the Political Bureau while Abu Marzouq was in prison, and since his release he has been acting as Mish'al's deputy. In 1999 the Jordanian authorities decided to close down Hamas's offices there, forcing him and other leaders to move to Syria, where officially he has remained up to the present.

Abu Marzouq is considered to be a pragmatist. Operational and a good organizer, he is reckless as well. His repeated visits to the United States exhibited carelessness and cost him dearly. He was also criticized in 1994 for what was known then as 'the Political Bureau (PB) Initiative' which was believed to have been his brainchild, offering Israel a solution that was based on the two-state concept, similar to what the PLO was calling for. Abu Marzouq's main points in the PB Initiative were:

1   The unconditional withdrawal of Zionist occupation forces from the West Bank and Gaza Strip, including Jerusalem.

2   The dismantling and removal of the settlements and the evacuation of settlers from the West Bank, Gaza Strip and Jerusalem.

3   The holding of free general elections for a legislative body among the Palestinian people inside and outside [Palestine] so that they can choose their own leaders and their real representatives. This legitimately elected leadership alone shall have the right to speak for our people's will and aspirations. It alone shall decide on all the subsequent steps in our struggle with the occupiers.

WHERE DOES HAMAS GET ITS MONEY?

There is of course very little public information about the finances or annual budget of Hamas. In recent years estimates have ranged from as modest a sum as US$10 million for the functioning of all aspects and branches of the organization, to as wild a projection as US$150 million. Perhaps contrary to the received wisdom created by the press, the smallest fraction of Hamas's budget is allocated to the military aspect. The lion's share actually goes to the social and welfare programmes that the movement provides to the Palestinians, especially the poor. These programmes, along with clean-handed administration and moral discipline, feed Hamas with sustained support and popularity among the Palestinians.

The sources of Hamas's funding, by the movement's own declarations, have been mostly donations coming from individual Palestinian, Arab and Muslim supporters of the movement. It is plausible to believe this claim given that neither Israel nor the United States has ever accused any state of funding Hamas, apart from Iran. Arab and Muslim countries, however, have been facing domestic pressure to support Hamas and the Palestinians, or at least to leave open the channels for popular support on a non-state basis. Thus countries in which potential

individual or organizational donors are being targeted by
Hamas for fundraising tend to turn a blind eye. In so doing the
governments of these countries are trying to stand on a middle
ground between strong local desires to donate money to Hamas,
and US pressure prohibiting direct state funding to Hamas.

Drying up Hamas's sources of money has always been a
high priority of Israeli and US policies. Even funds that were
clearly allocated for social services were targeted. The standard
Israeli and US claim is that the Islamic social welfare organizations that are controlled by Hamas in the West Bank and Gaza
Strip have been channelling funds to support the movement's
military activities. In fact the real purpose behind these
Israeli/US accusations is to close down these organizations altogether, to deny Hamas the immense credibility, political
currency and appreciation it draws from them. Thousands of
Palestinian families have been living for years on the monthly
support given by Hamas's social organizations. By the end of
the year 2003, and according to field data, these charities were
providing monthly financial assistance to 120,000 Palestinians,
with an additional 30,000 receiving help on an annual basis.

Hamas has also been successful in soliciting funds from
wealthy and middle-class Palestinians in the West Bank and the
Gaza Strip. Challenging harsh Israeli obstacles and the American and western international surveillance of any money that
could go to Hamas, the movement has prudently maintained
local sources of funding. In hundreds of mosques across Palestinian cities, Hamas supporters donate money that ends up
directly in the coffers of Hamas, funding its activities.

When Hamas came to power early in 2006, it faced the new
dilemma of securing enormous funds not for its own functioning, but to feed the entire Palestinian population, who were
stricken by increased rates of poverty and unemployment. A
concerted Israeli-US-European effort succeeded in cutting off
the supply of the annual Palestinian Authority operating funds
that the previous Fatah administration had received. Their goal

has been to bring Hamas's government to a complete collapse, and to teach the Palestinian people a lesson for electing Hamas in the first place. In the eyes of most Palestinians this international blocking of funds is a punishment against Palestinians for having exercised their free will in the democratic elections that were urged upon them. Ben Bot, the Dutch foreign minister, said on the eve of declaring the EU decision to halt European funds, 'The Palestinian people have opted for this government, so they will have to bear the consequences.'

10   A new Hamas?

HAMAS AND THE 2006 ELECTIONS

In the first 20 years of its existence, the undoubted turning point in Hamas's political life has been its unexpected victory in the January 2006 legislative elections in the West Bank and the Gaza Strip. Bringing about new realities and challenges, the significance of these elections is tantamount to a paradigm shift not only in the thinking and practice of the movement itself but also across the whole Palestinian political scene. (See Chapter 5.) A 'new discourse' had indeed been showing up in Hamas's thinking during the campaign for these elections and has not simply resulted from their victory in the elections per se. In fact Hamas was readjusting itself to this course of political action a few years back.

Why did Hamas as a resistance movement decide to compete for 'governmental power' in the West Bank and the Gaza Strip in 2006?

Understanding Hamas's road to the 2006 elections and subsequent power can be furthered by highlighting two main introductory points. The first pertains to the intellectual and ideological development and change in Hamas's political thinking over the past few years. The second deals with more recent events, and is directly connected to the significant March 2005 decision of Hamas to run for the Legislative Palestinian Council elections (along with other crucial decisions).

On the point of its intellectual and political evolution, Hamas has striven hard since its inception in late 1987 to harmonize two impetuses within the movement: the nationalist liberationist drive and the religious Islamist one (see Chapter 2). These two intellectual and mobilizational agendas were neither necessarily contradictory nor fully harmonious. They strode hand in hand at certain periods, clashed with each other at other times, or simply moved at different paces. Which one took the lead and when has depended on the conjunctural political conditions at any given time. Hamas is thus simultaneously a 'nationalist' and 'religious' movement, moulded in the broader Palestinian context whose compass is to liberate the Palestinians from the Israeli occupation. The 'nationalist' and 'religious' have largely overlapped, but sometimes could be seen as a continuum.

Similar to other Palestinian movements, such as Fatah, Hamas's ultimate nationalist aim is to 'liberate Palestine'. Unlike other movements, however, Hamas adopted an Islamist, rather than a secular, ideology in order to achieve this aim. Initially espousing the ideological objective of other classical movements of political Islam, namely the establishment of an Islamic state, Hamas's early rhetoric emphasized that once the 'liberation' of Palestine was achieved, the resulting Palestinian state would be an Islamic one. In later stages this rhetoric about the 'Islamic state' was toned down.

The tension between the 'nationalist' and the 'religious' tendencies within Hamas culminated in the idea of participation in the 2006 elections, and resulted from surrounding pressing conditions, which is the second introductory point to be made. The decision to run for the elections came about only after a traumatic birth in March 2005. In the minds of many Hamas supporters (and foes), the decision contrasted severely with Hamas's earlier rejection of any participation in similar elections in 1996. That rejection was based on the insistence that those elections were part and parcel of the Oslo Agreements of 1993–94 between the Palestine Liberation Organization (PLO) and Israel, which Hamas strongly opposed. The 2006 elections, practically speaking, were however organized within the political framework resulting from those agreements, hence the controversy within Hamas prior to its reaching the final decision to participate. In fact, the March 2005 decision was coupled with two equally significant decisions: the suspension of Hamas's suicide attacks against Israel and the agreement in principle to join the PLO. Hamas was thus making important leaps in the direction of playing a more political role, and reducing its military activities.

The military factor itself was a significant factor behind Hamas's decision to participate in an electoral process which would in fact legitimize the very same authority that Hamas has strongly opposed. In the years following the 2000 Intifada Hamas accumulated considerable military power; at the heart of it was the strong and well organized and armed military wing Izzeddin al-Qassam. In the very same years, however, the Palestinians became exhausted, harvesting no concrete achievements from either the peace talks track of Fatah and the Palestinian Authority (PA) or the resistance track of Hamas. Facing a visible impasse, and bearing the weight of its ever-growing mini army of more than 10,000 strong men, Hamas felt a pressing need to protect its military force by attaining further forms of legitimacy, within the system and not outside of it. Becoming part of the Legislative Council would enable Hamas to maintain its military wing, vetoing any potential measures to crack down on the resistance factions in general, unlike the paralysis that Hamas had suffered in the past when the PA took free rein in imposing crippling measures against any military activity. Thus, the engagement in the political process (through entering the Legislative Council) was envisaged by Hamas as a way of protecting its military capabilities, whether they are active or idle. A new Hamas had come into the making.

The decision to run for the elections was promptly translated into action. 'On the day following that decision,' as one of Hamas' leaders told me immediately after the announcement of the results of the elections, 'we immediately started practical preparation, wasting no time.' Hamas's campaign for the 2006 elections was organized under the heading of 'Change and Reform'. It issued a significant 'Electoral Platform' of 14 pages covering all political, social, educational, legal and environmental aspects. The most interesting dimension of this electoral platform was the deliberate minimization of the 'religiosity' of Hamas, allowing for more political and nationalist discourse. Most of Hamas's pronouncements in its electoral agenda came to fit neatly within the thinking of any other secular Palestinian faction.

What is the content and significance of Hamas's 'Electoral platform' for the 2006 elections

Demarcating the lines of 'newness' in Hamas's thinking, two significant election-born documents were issued by the movement: the 'Electoral platform for change and reform' upon which Hamas ran in the elections, and the 'Government platform', in which a victorious post-election Hamas suggested a basis for a national unity cabinet to other Palestinian factions in March 2006 (discussed below).

In the 'Electoral platform' Hamas incorporated the changes and experiences that had evolved in its organization over the past years, and showed how it had developed its perceptions, discourse and priorities. Measured against its original bold positions expressed in the early years of its inception, both in the Charter (discussed in Chapter 2) and elsewhere, the 'Electoral platform for change and reform' promoted an almost new Hamas. Yet drawing any conclusions about political parties based only on their electoral platforms can be misleading. Parties naturally try to draft their finest political statements at election time in order to attract as many voters as they can, and this electioneering rhetoric does not always reflect their real convictions and politics. Scepticism as a first impression is thus understandable when reading Hamas's carefully written electoral document, where the movement clearly was striving to tone down its controversial views, broaden its national appeal and reposition itself at the heart of mainstream Palestinian politics. This rhetoric will be examined against what Hamas was ready to offer in its cabinet programme, which is dealt with in the next chapter.

The significance of the 'Electoral platform' stems from several aspects. First, it provided the political justification for Hamas's own change in position regarding the very idea of participating in any electoral process that was initially a product of the Oslo Accords. Hamas opposed those Accords and never acknowledged the legitimacy of any measures or structures resulting from them, including the Legislative Council and its elections. On the basis of this, Hamas refused to participate in the first round of elections for the council in 1996.

The 'Electoral platform' for the 2006 Council explains that Hamas's participation in the elections 'takes place within a comprehensive programme for the liberation of Palestine and the return of the Palestinian people to their lands, and the establishment of an independent Palestinian state with Jerusalem as its capital'. It reiterates that 'this participation will support "resistance" as a strategic choice accepted by the Palestinian people to end the (Israeli) occupation'. In confirming these principles in the preamble of its electoral statement, Hamas was anxious to make a clear distinction between its participation and its rejection of the Oslo Accords. Knowing this distinction would not be fully convincing for many Palestinians because the Legislative Council itself is indivisible from the framework of Oslo Agreements, Hamas raised the tone of its rhetoric and asserted that its participation constituted a form of its wider 'resistance programme'. At the end of the long 14-page statement, Hamas made the even bolder statement that 'realities on the ground have made Oslo all but in the past ... all parties including the Zionist occupier speak about the demise of Oslo.'

Second, although the "Electoral platform' reiterated the conventional canons of Hamas thinking and outlook regarding the struggle against the Israeli occupation, it did so in more nuanced language than previously. For example, there was neither talk about the 'destruction of Israel' – an eye-catching phrase that has been used repeatedly by the press to describe Hamas's ultimate goal – nor any mention of establishing an Islamic state in Palestine. Instead, the discourse of the platform focused on 'ending the occupation', a term that cut consistently throughout the length of the document. On two occasions this document borrowed the language of old documents. The first came in the preamble, which stated that Hamas's participation in the elections was an integral part of 'the wider programme for the liberation of Palestine', and the second was mentioned in the first article, which confirmed that 'historic Palestine is part of Arab and Muslim lands, and irrefutably belongs to the Palestinian people'. One could safely argue that these declarations were meant to sustain continuity with the old discourse of the movement, and represent more rhetoric than politics. This is fairly demonstrated in that the rest of the document offered no mechanisms to implement these goals, as was the case with other detailed and pragmatic declarations in the statement.

Third, in the 'Electoral platform' document Hamas gave considerable focus to the themes of 'change and reform', reflected as they are in the very name of its platform of issues for the elections. In fact it was rather surprising that Hamas, as a self-defined resistance movement with a military/jihadist outlook, chose such a mild theme and name for its election campaign. However, there was no lack of cleverness in concentrating on 'change and reform' against a backdrop of its corrupt and failed Fatah rival, and Hamas's electoral platform effectively relegated 'military resistance' to the back seat. There is simply no comparison between the weight and detail given to civilian aspects of governance promised by Hamas in this document, and the weight and detail given to 'military resistance'. Attempting to link the urgency of internal reform with the wider cause of the struggle against the Israeli occupation, Hamas stated that:

> Change and reform will endeavour to build an advanced Palestinian civil society based on political pluralism and the rotation of power. The political system of this society and its reformist and political agenda will be oriented toward achieving Palestinian national rights.

Fourth, the 'Electoral platform' significantly provided the broadest vision that Hamas had ever presented concerning all aspects of Palestinian life. Throughout the detailed 18 articles, Hamas covered virtually every aspect of the societal and political setting of the Palestinians. It outlined what it would do if it won the elections in areas including resistance to the occupation, internal affairs, foreign affairs, administration reform and fighting corruption, judicial reform and policies, public liberties and individual rights, educational policy, religious guidance, social policy, cultural and media policy, youth issues, housing policy, health and environmental policy, agricultural policy, economic, financial and fiscal policies, labour issues, and issues over transportation and passage between Gaza and the West Bank.

Hamas had never before tackled such a wide-ranging spectrum of issues. Typically, Hamas (as well as other Islamist movements) has been accused of lack of pragmatic political vision: its rhetoric and mobilization override practical programmes and detailed perceptions. It is clear that this accusation was in the mind of the Hamas members who drafted its 'Electoral platform'. Compared with previous pivotal documents issued since its inception (such as the Charter in 1988 and the 'Introductory memorandum' in 1993), this document moved Hamas further into the realm of realistic politics, yet without diminishing the visible dose of religious and cultural mobilization that had been injected into it.

Fifth, Hamas's 'Electoral platform' also implied elements of what could be interpreted as its tacit desire, combined with quiet effort, to achieve the Islamization of society. These elements were received negatively by many secular Palestinians and others. Hamas persistently justifies this stance by arguing that these aspects reflect the true aspirations of society. Many people vote for Hamas at least partly because of these aspects, and the sector of Hamas's electorate who do not are fully aware of the presence of these aspects in the movement's programme, to varying degrees of controversy. Among these aspects is the confirmation that Islam is 'our frame of reference and the system of all political, economic, social and legal aspects of life'. Other articles stipulate that 'Islamic sharia law should be the principal source of legislation in Palestine', which is a somewhat standard and controversial statement existing in the constitutions of all Arab and Muslim countries. In this clause and similar ones the point of controversy is over whether sharia law should be the 'sole and ultimate source', or 'one of the' sources of legislation.

In the articles that dealt with education and social aspects, Hamas's 'Electoral platform' emphasized that the values of Islam should be respected and included because they provide strength and wholesomeness to society. For secular Palestinians, an even more worrying statement occurred in the context of tackling cultural and media provision, stressing the need for 'fortifying citizens, especially the youth, from corruption, westernization and intellectual penetration'.[1]

---

1   For extended analysis of Hamas's Electoral Platform, see Khaled Hroub (2006), 'A "new Hamas" through its new documents', *Journal of Palestine Studies*, No. 4, Summer, pp. 6–28.

THE SIGNIFICANCE OF HAMAS'S VICTORY IN THE LEGISLATIVE COUNCIL ELECTIONS OF 2006

On 25 January 2006 Hamas, which is still officially branded as a terrorist organization by the United States and the European Union, won the Legislative Council elections and became in charge of the Palestinian Authority. It achieved this stunning triumph against the wishes (and efforts) of many parties: its main rival Fatah (of the PLO), Israel, the United States, the European Union, the United Nations and a number of Arab countries. Harvesting an unexpected victory in the elections, Hamas faced a situation for which it had never been prepared: forming a Palestinian government. The movement had long trained its candidates for the Legislative Council to function as an opposition, not a ruling party. After its unexpected victory Hamas immediately chose to call upon all other Palestinian factions to join it in a coalition government. Leaders of the movement spent almost two months trying to convince other parties to join them. As had been expected Fatah refused the offer, hoping that an 'inexperienced' Hamas at the top of the Palestinian Authority would quickly fail, which would bring Fatah back to power. Leftist Palestinian factions and other independent personalities equally rejected Hamas's offer, protesting against the 'government political programme'. Their position was hardened by Hamas's refusal to declare bluntly in the government programme that the PLO was the sole and legitimate representative of the Palestinian people. In the end, on 29 March, Hamas formed an exclusive government of its own members and close supporters.

In response to Hamas's government the Quartet (the United States, the European Union, Russia and the United Nations) imposed three conditions before they would establish normal relations (and provide aid) with the government: recognition of Israel, acknowledgement of all previous agreements between the Palestinian Authority and Israel, and a complete stop to 'terrorism'. The three conditions were rejected by Hamas. Western and non-Western diplomatic relations with the Hamas government were either immediately severed or not established. In the following months, and apart from a very few countries, Hamas ministers were unwelcome almost everywhere. Many Arab and Muslim countries had carefully synchronized their moves towards the Hamas government with Western policies. The immediate and disastrous outcome of the resulting embargo placed on the government was felt most catastrophically at the level of ordinary Palestinians. European and other international funding to the Palestinian Authority, which is one of the two main sources of income for Palestinian public life, was stopped. The second main source of income, the monthly Palestinian tax revenues controlled and collected by Israel, in accordance with the Oslo Agreements, were also frozen.[2] Caught between the hammer of rising internal dissatisfaction and the anvil of external embargo, Hamas's policies started to grow nervous. Yet the movement and its government has also demonstrated a great level of steadfastness and remained intact and coherent.

In addition to facing the cutting-off of all funds, the Hamas-led government had to endure continuous Israeli military pressure and incursions into areas of the West Bank and the Gaza Strip. At the risk of erosion of its own 'resistance legitimacy', Hamas leaders pressured its military wing to exercise restraint and to maintain the shaky truce (*hudna*) that

---

2 In the year 2005, according to the World Bank statistics, the PA expenditure was US$1.92 billion, of which international aid provided $349 million whereas the tax and customs transfers controlled by Israel accounted for $814 million. See World Bank, *Coping with Crisis: Palestinian Authority Institutional Performance,* Jerusalem, November 2006.

had been in place since months prior to the elections. But at the same time they allowed other factions, such as Islamic Jihad, to resume launching rockets and conducting other military activities in response to the relentless Israeli raids against the Gaza Strip.

At a factional level Fatah, which had been defeated in the elections, decided to make Hamas's time in government as difficult as possible. The goal, whether overtly stated or covertly planned, was to foil Hamas in power and force it to step down, resulting in a need for early new elections. Because of Fatah's domination over the Palestinian civil service by virtue of its control of the Palestinian Authority during the previous 12 years, tensions between the new Hamas ministers and their Fatah staff paralysed the work of many ministries and the public sector in general. On the security front, and particularly in the Gaza Strip, several Fatah-controlled security organizations remained outside the control of the Hamas interior ministry, making the government appear to be toothless. To compensate for this awkward situation of having the security forces out of governmental control, the interior ministry established its own 'official' security apparatus, the 'Executive Force'. Predictably, a growing friction between this new force (most of whose members were drawn from Hamas) and the old Fatah-controlled forces continued to increase, leading to military clashes between the two parties during January and February and then again in May and June 2007, pushing the situation in the Gaza Strip to the brink of an all-out civil war. This was only briefly averted in early 2007 by the sudden heavyweight intervention of the Saudis, culminating in the Mecca Agreement between Fatah and Hamas in February 2007. Based on this agreement a 'national unity government' was formed. However it failed after only three months when Hamas took over all the security strongholds of Fatah in June 2007. This is further discussed below.

What are the implications of Hamas's victory for the Palestinian polity and legitimacy?

At the level of Hamas as a movement and in the eyes of Palestinians at large, Hamas's victory in the elections and the subsequent formation of its government brought about new realities. For the first time in the history of the Palestinian national movement, a party that subscribed to Islamist/religious ideology had managed to eclipse all other secular factions, leftists and nationalists allied together, and advanced to the forefront. This dramatic change challenged the traditional leadership of 'the Palestinian nationalist liberationist project' which had been controlled almost entirely by secular forces since the days of the British Mandate in the 1920s.

Furthermore, Hamas's 2006 victory meant that the legitimacy of the historical 'Palestinian leadership' of the PLO was contested on all fronts: in terms of armed resistance, popular representation, and trust and credibility. If embracing and practising 'resistance' against the Israeli occupation was the source of popular legitimacy for any Palestinian faction, Hamas not only achieved that but also garnered a democratic victory that bestowed on it unprecedented moral and political leverage.

Hamas's triumph also accentuated the dichotomy in Palestinian politics between itself and Fatah. The weakness of other factions with either leftist or liberal orientations was further exposed. In many ways, this was an unfortunate development that can be attributed in large measure to the disorientation that many Palestinian elites had and have suffered before, during and after the Oslo Agreements. Suffice it to say in this respect that in light of the sharp Fatah/Hamas polarity, the chances of the emergence of a popular and powerful 'third way' in Palestinian politics are slim for the foreseeable future. After one year of Hamas rule, the formation of a national unity government in March 2007 could have represented a historic milestone in Palestinian politics. In fact, the agreement could have helped create a political consensus upon which the Palestinians could deal with Israel, thus bridging the destructive gulf that has so far crippled Palestinian political thinking and strategy.

Over the past 15 years or so, Palestinian forces have been divided between two strategies for achieving Palestinian rights and self-determination: peace talks with Israel (the stance of the PLO and the Palestinian Authority) or military resistance against the Israeli occupation (Hamas and other factions). Both strategies worked against Israel but also against each other, yielding little for the Palestinians. Because they worked in opposing directions, these two strategies have effectively frustrated one another: what might have been achieved by one of them would be wasted by the opposite party. The lack of a unified leadership (and vision) that could harmonize the duality of 'resistance and negotiation' resulted in the dynamism of mutual destruction between the two opposing strategies. Sustaining a united platform as embodied in the national unity government could be seen therefore as a necessity for internal coherence of the Palestinian national movement and the resolution of the conflict with Israel. External actors certainly have helped in the early collapse of the national unity government and the potential of long-term consensus-building among the Palestinians. The continuation of economic and financial embargos on the national unity government and the explicit policy of sustaining Mahmoud Abbas against Hamas caused the resumption of clashes between Hamas and Fatah and the collapse of the National Unity Government by June 2007. Not only did Western and Israeli policies provoke the return of a destructive polarity in the Palestinian national movement, they also encouraged the formation and reformation of smaller militant groups which listen neither to Fatah nor to Hamas.

What are the implications for Israel and for the future of a peace settlement?

The ramifications of Hamas's electoral victory on the Israeli–Palestinian conflict could be examined by addressing two main questions. First, would Hamas in power help or hinder the achievement of a peace settlement? And two, would Hamas in power pose more or less of a threat to Israel's security and citizens?

Concerning the first question it is necessary to clarify some assumptions. Before and during Hamas's taking power there have been no genuine peace talks in motion to be helped or hindered by Hamas. The peace track had gone astray well before Hamas's rise to power. Since the second *intifada*, in 2000, which erupted in response to Oslo's failure to bring about any tangible gains for the Palestinians, the peace process had effectively been idle. Although Mahmoud Abbas had been the leader of the Palestinians for more than a year before the 2006 elections, and is still at the top of the Palestinian polity hierarchy, Israel has not engaged with him in serious negotiations. Abbas is seen as the most moderate Palestinian leader with whom Israel could (or should) make peace. Yet he was considered to be incompetent as a 'peace partner' by Israel, and his political capital in the eyes of the Palestinians has gradually been eroded as he failed to change their dire status quo.

Furthermore and regardless of the internal make-up of the Palestinian government, there have been strong doubts whether the Israeli side is ready to make any serious moves towards concluding a peace agreement. The current Israeli leadership has been somewhat damaged politically and humiliated militarily after the Lebanon war in summer 2006, and in addition a number of top Israeli figures have faced prosecution for financial or sexual corruption. If the Ehud Olmert government were forced to resign, any potential alternative – either another Kadima-led government, potentially as weak as the current one, or a Netanyahu/Lieberman-led government, representing the far right – would not be expected to gear up the agenda for any peace process with the Palestinians. Therefore it really remains an open question whether Hamas should be held responsible for the 'inaction' of the peace talks between the two parties. It is worth noting that after the Annapolis Conference (held in November 2007 in the United States, which relaunched negotiations between the Israelis and the Palestinians), talks between the Israelis and the Palestinians in December 2007 faced intractable difficulties, not because of Hamas, but because of Israel's insistence on building new settlement units in East Jerusalem.

In terms of military threat or security for Israel there is an apparent irony: the period in which Hamas was either in full control of the Palestinian Authority or engaged in power-sharing with Fatah (March 2006–June 2007) was almost the most peaceful and calm period that Israeli cities had enjoyed over the past few years. The year running up to the elections and the year of Hamas in power witnessed almost zero suicide attacks conducted by Hamas in Israel. Here, Hamas's pragmatism again was in the lead, and realistic cost–benefit calculations overrode religious or Jihad calls for unguided resistance.

Another security scenario that could be contemplated, which is largely related to changes within and surrounding Hamas, is the possibility of the emergence of al-Qaeda cells within the Palestinian territories. This could be the result of a combination of several factors. Among these is the appeal to angry and frustrated Palestinian factions of the uncompromising al-Qaeda model which has been embraced in Iraq and elsewhere in the world. This might also be true for the many disenfranchised ultra-religious zealots within Hamas, who have become disillusioned by the 'futile' political line adopted by their leadership. These factors are exacerbated by the chaotic situation in the Gaza Strip in particular and the free market of arms. Nonetheless, so far and perhaps against all favourable conditions, al-Qaeda has failed to establish its own cells in Palestine. Hamas has functioned as a bulwark blocking any newly emerging group, and al-Qaeda has found it hard to infiltrate. However, things could start to change. The erroneous external policies by Israel and the West in general that have placed the Gaza Strip under blockade, starving people and humiliating them, will naturally provoke more radical tendencies than the already existing ones.

11   Hamas in power

THE MIXED FORTUNES OF HAMAS IN POWER

At the time of updating this book, after its electoral victory and the formation of an exclusive Hamas-led government in March 2006, which was followed by a short-lived national unity government (in March 2007), then a military takeover of the Gaza Strip in June 2007, the balance sheet of Hamas's performance is mixed. Notwithstanding that central to the tremendous difficulties that Hamas has faced is the international and regional blockade imposed on its government and the cutting-off of aid and diplomatic relations with the Palestinians, Hamas in power, as opposed to Hamas in opposition, has structurally changed the rules of the game in the Palestinian–Israeli conflict. Hamas, acknowledged as a major party on the Palestinian political scene, has now become an integral part of the Palestinian leadership. Without its participation, or tacit approval at the very least, any lasting peace agreement between the two sides seems to be inconceivable.

Hamas's experience in power moved from forming an exclusive government, to participating in a national unity government, to military control of the Gaza Strip. Each of these episodes deserves a closer look.

*What is the content and significance of the Hamas
'Government platform'?*

Perhaps more important than Hamas's 'Electoral platform',
discussed in Chapter 10, is the 'Government platform' delivered by Hamas's Prime Minster Ismail Haniya on 27 March
2006 before the newly elected parliament, in which he asked
it to furnish his cabinet with a vote of confidence. In this
highly significant statement, Hamas was addressing the entire
world in new and carefully crafted language. Obviously, it
was an audacious undertaking by Hamas to try to appeal to a
host of completely different audiences. It had to live up to its
promises and the expectations of its own membership, and to
appease the wider Palestinian constituencies, in particular
reassuring Fatah and other big losers in the elections. It also
had to send the right and definitive message to Israel and
beyond, that Hamas is not a belligerent and war-loving movement. The statement thus projected a moderate discourse with
the hope of having an impact on international (mainly American and European) audiences who were shocked and
displeased by Hamas's victory. Concurrently, the statement
had to appease and assure other Islamist movements and
exponents of political Islam in the Middle East and beyond
that the Hamas in power was and would be the same Hamas
that they had always known. At the same time, it was essential
that Hamas portray itself as a responsible moderate government, trustworthy to its neighbouring sceptical Arab regimes,
which feared the ramifications of Hamas's victory on their
domestic affairs.

As tedious a statement as it might seem to be, drafting the
'Government platform' was indeed an exercise in reconciling
somewhat irreconcilable concerns and parties. Nonetheless, it
has represented a true turning point in Hamas's political
thinking. In it, Hamas tackled the conflict with Israel in a
language that was borrowed from international law and
conventions. It focused on the fact that the Palestinians suffer

from the Israeli military occupation, and thus they have a legitimate right to resist it by all means. The entire thrust of the statement was confined directly and indirectly to the parameters of the concept of a two-state solution. There was no mention or even the slightest of a hint of the 'destruction of Israel' or the establishment of an 'Islamic state in Palestine'. It reflected very little inclination to radical positions and religious overtones. Someone who read this statement without knowing it had been produced by Hamas could justifiably think that it had been written by any secular Palestinian organization.

At the beginning of his speech, Haniya made a clear reference to the fact that his government would operate 'according to the articles of the basic law modified in 2003'. Referring to the 'basic law' was clearly extremely significant because this law was rooted in and developed on the basis of, and because of, the Oslo Accords. Legally and literally speaking, Hamas was functioning within the parameters created by the peace talks between Israel and the Palestine Liberation Organization (PLO), which it vehemently opposed.

The 'Government platform' stipulated seven major challenges that would make up the government's agenda:

First, resisting the occupation and its oppressive undertakings against the [Palestinian] land, its people, resources and holy places. Second, securing the safety of the Palestinians and ending the security chaos. Third, relieving the economic hardships facing the Palestinian people. Fourth, undertaking reform and fighting financial and administrative corruption. Five, reordering internal Palestinian affairs by reorganizing Palestinian institutions on a democratic basis that would guarantee political participation for all. Sixth, strengthening the status of the Palestinian question in Arabic and Muslim circles. Seventh, developing Palestinian relationships at regional and international levels to further serve the ultimate interests of our people.

With the 'Government platform' Haniya called upon the international community to respect the choice of the Palestinians in electing Hamas, and to reconsider the initial negative responses to the Hamas victory. He also assured international donors who had been complaining about the corrupt management of the Palestinian Authority that any new aid would be spent through the right channels, and invited donors to establish whatever monitoring mechanisms they considered necessary to guarantee the proper expenditure of their money in Palestine.

On the United States and its position on Hamas's government, the document stated that:

> the American administration which has been preaching democracy and the respect of people's choices across the world is required before anyone else to support the will and choice of the Palestinian people. Instead of threatening the Palestinians with boycotts and cutting aid it should fulfil the pledges that it made to help the establishment of an independent Palestinian state with Jerusalem as its capital.

Pertaining to the major rights of Palestinians, the statement stressed 'upholding the rights of Palestinian refugees to return to their homeland and for compensation, for this right is indelible and uncompromisable at the individual and collective level'. It also declared the government's commitment to work to free (about 8–9,000) Palestinian prisoners from Israeli jails, defend Jerusalem against Judaization and challenge all manner of collective punishments against the Palestinians.

On the peace agreements signed by the PLO or the former Fatah-led government and Israel, the statement

assured 'other parties' that the government would treat those
agreements:

> with high national responsibility, and in ways that
> assist the interest of our people and their unchange-
> able prerogatives. It will also deal with the UN reso-
> lutions [on Palestine/Israel] with a high sense of
> national responsibility and in ways that protect the
> rights of our people.

The statement addressed at length, and with pride, the Palestinian exercise of democracy, and confirmed the government's
adherence to that concept. It stated that 'as this government is
a result of fair and free elections' it would adhere to the
'democratic choice', protecting Palestinian democracy and
the peaceful rotation of power. It would also broaden the platform of political participation and pluralism because these are
the guarantors of the sound functioning and stability of our
political system'.

It is noteworthy that this document, which was produced
by a religiously oriented movement which has been seen to be
cultivating its popularity on the basis of primordial alle-
giances, criticized all sorts of non-citizenship affiliation. It
declared that the government would work to get rid of tribal
and provincial loyalties and instead 'would encourage the
concepts of citizenship and equality of rights and duties'. The
notion of citizenship was emphasized as being the overriding
one over other local, tribal or religious affiliations:

> we will protect the rights of citizens and strengthen
> the concept of citizenship without any discrimination
> based on creed or political association, and will
> fight together against the practice of political or
> professional exclusion, and will struggle against [any]
> injustices inflicted on people.

References to 'good governance' were plentiful, covering a wide range of issues:

> the government will fight corruption and the misuse of public money and confirm transparency and fairness ... [and will adopt] new strategies to develop a public administration based on modern concepts of management.

On the economic side of Hamas's 'Government platform', free-market thinking was visibly expressed, but with a close eye to social justice and care for the poor. But it started by emphasizing self-reliance within the constraints imposed by the Israeli occupation:

> our economic programme strives to achieve sustainable development through the release of our own [national] resources and by making the best use of our fortunes. We are aware, however, of the political restrictions and the effects of occupation that besiege our people and which have caused drastic damage to our infrastructure.

The statement then moved on to encourage Arab, Muslim and other business groups to come to Palestine and explore investment opportunities, promising that 'we will make available to them all help possible toward creating the appropriate investment climate including safety, economic protection and the issuing of necessary regulations'. It also stressed the role of such foreign investment as opposed to external donations, stating that:

> investment is one of the underpinnings of sustainable development, where aid should not be relied on entirely, although this aid is necessary at this period of time. One

of the utmost priorities of our economic programme is to encourage investment in Palestine, and our government will be actively ready to negotiate all the details that are required by foreign investment.

How was the performance of the year-long Hamas-led government?

The balance sheet of Hamas's one year in power offers a melange of success and failure. It is important to point out from the beginning, however, that a considerable part of Hamas's failure can be attributed to the embargo and aid suspension imposed on the government by the international community. In the eyes of many Palestinians, Hamas was partly, if not largely, absolved of much responsibility for failing to deliver public services, which were largely crippled by its failure to pay the salaries of more than 160,000 civil servants. This failure was blamed on Western and Israeli policies, which were seen as a punishment against all Palestinians because of their democratic choice of Hamas.[1] But at the level of Hamas as a political movement, the experience was, and is still, painfully diverse. A frequent sentiment heard from Hamas's leaders about their time in power revolves around what Ahmad Yousef, the political advisor to the Hamas-appointed prime minister Ismail Haniya, told me in March 2007, that 'it was a tough year but a great one as well; like an intensive course on politics where we had to learn in one year what would otherwise take us 10 or 15 years to learn'.

During Hamas's year in power, one of the several remarkable and speedy transformations that took place within the movement's discourse was the shift in its *justification* of its

---

1   Ben Bot, the Dutch foreign minister, was quoted on the record saying, 'The Palestinian people have opted for this government, so they will have to bear the consequences' (Associated Press, 10 April 2007).

'hard-line' positions. Religious justifications and rhetoric increasingly gave way to political justifications and discourse. The increasing exposure to politics and the outside world engendered a discourse that was formulated more in accordance with external conditions rather than being shaped by unfettered internal ideological thinking. This further confirms the predominance of the nationalist pragmatic line in Hamas over the religious one in recent years. Hamas in power felt the burning need to repackage its positions in a more political format. While this could appear to have been a surface change, it nonetheless permeated deeper into the layers of the political and ideological thinking of Hamas. The impact of such a discourse of *justification* would prove to be most considerable among the lower ranks of the movement, where the religiosity was stronger and rigidity of thinking more apparent. External factors would play a significant role in this context, in transforming what could have been a mere passing momentary shift into deeply rooted change. It was thus the set of surrounding political and social conditions with their pressures and dictats that would ultimately determine Hamas's responses and shift.

Examples of this shift are many, yet it is sufficient to highlight three major ones that have immediate relevance to current debates about Hamas and its changing fortunes. The first example is the question of recognizing Israel. Hamas's 'starting position' on this question was purely religious. Recognizing Israel was perceived to be tantamount to an infringement of Islam, and thus was considered to lie beyond the practice of politics. Hamas's Charter was blunt in denouncing any party, Palestinian, Arab or Muslim that would undertake such an anti-religious stance. Palestine was declared to be a *waqf* or an endowment for Muslim generations with which no one has the right to compromise. The justification that today's Hamas would offer on the same position, however, is political and not a religious one. Hamas argues that Israel is a 'borderless' state and that it has never identified clear borders. So what is the geography of

Israel, Hamas's leaders would now ask, that the movement and the Palestinians are asked to recognize? Hamas's spokesmen also contend that the PLO has recognized Israel since 1988 yet this has not brought any tangible benefits for the Palestinians. Hamas leaders point to the Arab Summit Peace Initiative adopted in Beirut in 2002, which offered Israel full and collective Arab recognition and normalization of relations in return for accepting the two-state solution according to UN resolutions. Their point is that when Israel refuses such a collective Arab recognition, how and why would Hamas's recognition of Israel change Israel's attitudes and positions?[2]

The second example of the change in the justification used by Hamas regarding its position relates to the movement's policy of suspending military attacks in Israeli cities, before and after the elections. This policy, rigidly and religiously speaking, is akin to stopping the *jihad*, the *raison d'être* of Hamas. Perhaps no other notion was more repeatedly confirmed in Hamas's early literature in the late 1980s and early 1990s than that of *jihad*. Yet when Hamas is now asked why it has frozen its *jihad* against Israel, it resorts to political and not to religious justifications. Its leaders link this decision to the delicate calculations that account for the unfavourable political conditions of Hamas's position as a government. The significance of such thinking denotes the extent to which Hamas is willing to subjugate its ideological, and seemingly inflexible, convictions to its political pragmatism and goals. Hamas's rhetoric still stresses

2   These statements have been repeatedly expressed by Hamas leaders' statements and written articles. For example, see Ismail Haniya's 'A just peace or no peace', *Guardian*, 31 March 2006; Musa Abu Marzuk, 'What Hamas is seeking', *Washington Post*, 31 January 2006; and statements made by Khaled Mish'al, Hamas's political bureau chief, to *Al-Quds Al-Arabi*, 28 February 2007. By contrast, statements that would refer to religious qualification of this position have dramatically diminished.

the concept of 'resistance', even when this 'resistance' is effectively idle. More significant is the new confirmation that resistance is a political means and not an objective in itself. Or, in the words of Khaled Mish'al, the head of Hamas's political bureau, 'resistance is not an end in itself, but a means to an end' (quoted in a 17 March 2007 interview).

The third example that underlines the shift in Hamas's political thinking in terms of offering political rather than religious qualification of its practices is the movement's stance towards the PLO and the question of joining this organization. The PLO has been the embodiment of Palestinian legitimacy and representation for many decades, recognized as the sole and legitimate representative of the Palestinians. Established in 1964, and controlled by Fatah, the main Palestinian nationalist movement, all Palestinian factions, nationalist, Marxist and pan-Arabist, joined the organization at different points in time, seeing it as the umbrella for Palestinian nationalist resistance against Zionist aggression in Palestine.

Hamas, the late-comer to the resistance scene in 1987, neither joined the PLO nor acknowledged it as 'the sole' representative of the Palestinian people. It considered the PLO only as 'a' representative of the Palestinians. One of its main objections to the PLO was its 'secular nature'. It was indeed seen as the antithesis of Hamas, the latter being a religious organization. Other main objections presented by Hamas included the PLO's tacit recognition of Israel by endorsing the principle of the two-state solution. Yet the position of today's Hamas concerning the PLO is different, or at least the justification of the old positions has changed. Further, Hamas has engaged in dialogue with Fatah and other Palestinian factions to reform the PLO and include Hamas in it. In all the discussions and debates about a 'new' PLO, which would include Hamas, there has not been a single statement or condition pronounced by any Hamas leader about the 'secular nature' of the PLO or its 'un-Islamic essence'. All the talk is political. Even the recognition of Israel by the PLO has been downplayed in view of the fact that Hamas's recent positions over the past few years have also been converging on the idea of the two-state solution.

THE MIXED FORTUNES OF HAMAS IN POWER SHARING AND CONTROL

What was the national unity government (and the agreement with Fatah) of March 2007 and why did it fail?

The rivalry between Fatah and Hamas since the January 2006 election results has pushed the internal Palestinian situation from bad to worse. By January 2007, marking exactly one full year since Hamas's victory, the spectre of civil war had become a serious potentiality as it never had been before in recent Palestinian history. Egyptian, Syrian, Qatari and Jordanian attempts to mediate between the two fighting factions had failed one after the other. In early February the Saudi King Abdallah took the initiative and called the leaders of both movements to convene in Mecca.

The Saudi initiative was successful, and between 6 and 8 February 2007 Fatah and Hamas concluded what would be known as the 'Mecca Agreement'. Putting an immediate end to Palestinian in-fighting in the Gaza Strip, the agreement paved the way for the formation of a Palestinian national unity government, which took place in March 2007. The political programme of the would-be government confirmed the pragmatic line of Hamas, in which it agreed to 'respect' previous agreements signed between the PLO and Israel. It also stipulated the establishment of a Palestinian state using the 1967 borders as the national aim of the government, yet without conceding a blunt recognition of Israel. The Mecca Agreement was a breakthrough, offering a potential Palestinian consensus, however shaky, on a unified political programme (see also Chapter 10 on the implications of Hamas's victory for the Palestinian polity and legitimacy).

The national unity government did not change the Quartet

and Israeli policies of isolating and boycotting Hamas. In particular the new government did not succeed on two fronts: breaking the international boycott and unifying the internal security forces under the control of the interior ministry. The skirmishes between Fatah-affiliated groups and security forces and Hamas's Executive Force and al-Qassam Brigades intensified. A new round of violent internal fighting in May and early June culminated in mid-June with Hamas's taking control of the security forces in the Gaza Strip. Dozens of Palestinians from both sides were killed, and hundreds wounded. The Gaza Strip fell entirely under Hamas control. Immediately after that Abbas nominated a non-Hamas government in the West Bank, which was quickly recognized and supported by the Quartet and by Israel. Since then the Palestinian polity and society and geography have come to an unprecedented divide, where the West Bank is under the control of Fatah and the Gaza Strip under the control of Hamas, and each claims to be the legitimate government. The 'international community' sided with the government in the West Bank, and tightened the blockade on Hamas and the Gaza Strip, and its almost one and a half million Palestinians.

Why did Hamas take over the Gaza Strip by force in June 2007?

The military takeover of the Gaza Strip can only be understood from the perspective of rational-players' power politics. Hamas and Fatah were stubbornly engaged in a rivalry over power, where the surrounding conditions would allow for the use of force more than reconciliation. On Fatah's side, and despite the fact that this occurred a year and a half into Hamas's electoral mandate, Fatah still considered it to be merely a short interruption to the 'natural course' of Palestinian leadership, with Fatah always at the helm. Fatah and the Palestinian president have spared no tactic to bring about the failure of the Hamas government. In the two weeks following the results of the elections, several presidential decrees were quickly issued, aimed at stripping basic powers from Hamas's government-in-waiting. Abbas brought back to the 'presidency' all the powers that he himself had struggled hard to wrest from the former president Yasser Arafat when he was prime minister in 2003. The 'presidency' started to accumulate excessive power, which had Hamas not been in government would have been criticized world-wide. Hamas's incoming government and its ministries were stripped of real authority, especially in the areas of finance and security, even before they assumed any responsibilities.

All security forces would, by virtue of the new decrees, be the responsibility of the president himself, and would be run by the National Security Council, which had played only a consultative role until it was reactivated after Hamas's victory. Official media, mainly Palestinian television, radio and the Palestinian news agency, were moved from under the jurisdiction of the Ministry of Information and became the responsibility of the presidency. All border points, especially the Rafah border (with Egypt), which had been under the control of the national security forces, belonging to the Interior Ministry, were brought under the authority of the presidency through its 'presidential guards'. The latter had rapidly been beefed up to become a most important military force, assuming far more responsibilities than safeguarding the president. A number of presidential decisions were also taken in which Fatah officials were appointed or promoted to occupy key security posts, so that it would be almost impossible for the incoming movement to take control over security. Even since the formation of the national unity government in March 2007, the failure to resolve the thorniest of issues, the control over security forces, has only confirmed the coming prospect of use of force by Hamas.

On Hamas's side the mounting pressures were also eliminating any alternatives but the resort to force to restructure the status quo. Because of its lack of control over security forces, Hamas's government failed in maintaining security for ordinary Palestinians, leaving the streets of the Gaza Strip to fall into the hands of

various groups of thugs and militant gangs. The chaotic situation
was partly provoked by militant elements affiliated either to Fatah
or to the 'official' apparatus of the Preventative Security. Their
aim was to prove that Hamas was incapable of delivering security,
discrediting it in the eyes of the Palestinians. Muhammad Dahlan,
Fatah's strongest man in the Gaza Strip, was reported stating on
the record that he would 'drive Hamas's government nuts'. Also,
and as a result of cutting off external aid, Hamas had failed to
provide salaries to tens of thousands of public sector employees.
Exploiting the situation, Fatah mobilized widespread strikes
among civil servants, especially teachers, which have truly
harmed Hamas's image. The compounded pressures on Hamas
created panic and unrest among the rank and file of the movement. The wisdom of engaging in such a political process, as
opposed to remaining on the 'resistance' and opposition side,
came into deep question.

Internally, anger and impatience were increasingly dominat-
ing Hamas's ever-growing military wing, which until then had
been kept under the full control of the political leadership. In the
days preceding the military takeover, Hamas's military had been
caught in a feeling of compounded humiliation. On the one hand,
and in order to avoid harming the political agenda of Hamas's
government, they had ceased their attacks against Israeli targets
which had fallen easily within their reach and capacity. This had
invoked criticism and mockery of their 'resistance project'; Fatah
was prompt in pointing at 'Hamas's relinquishing of resistance
for the sake of governmental posts'. On the other hand, the
chaotic security situation spreading across the Gaza Strip was
seen to be mobilized by their rival groups, from or close to Fatah,
which Hamas's military wing felt they could have ended if they
were only given the green light. Hamas's al-Qassam Brigades
were not allowed to interfere in the daily business of the government, although Hamas oversaw and trained the Executive Force,
which the government did establish to function as a police force.

Hamas's military wing by then had started to see itself as an impotent or put-to-pasture army, losing its respect and aura.

However, the most intolerable and decisive factor for Hamas's military leadership was the continuous arming of Abbas's presidential guards and other security forces in the Gaza Strip. Shipments of arms arrived in the Strip from Egypt, Jordan and Israel. For Hamas's military it looked as if they were merely naively waiting for their rivals to reach their military threshold, the point when it would be practically feasible for them to crush Hamas. They argued that it was necessary to take preventive action to save the movement from this almost inevitable scenario. For many of Hamas's military leadership it was a life or death decision, defending their very existence. It was them and their soldiers who would be on the 'wanted list' or even killed, not their political leadership which could coexist with others and live with the new status quo.

In a nutshell Hamas's government was put under enormous pressures externally, internally and organizationally. Cut off financially and diplomatically, 18 months after assuming power Hamas lacked any political capital to present to its own members or the Palestinian people at large. It was made to look crippled in delivering even the most conventional responsibilities of any government. On top of that, its military leadership perceived a ticking clock that would lead to the eventual destruction of the military power that they had spent years in building. All those pressures culminated in the political leadership giving way, perhaps for the first time in Hamas's political life, to its military wing, to decide how to deal with Fatah on the ground and implement these decisions. In November 2007 Hamas issued what it called the 'White Paper' [Al-Kitab al-Abyad], in which it explained its reasons behind the 'military takeover' of the Gaza Strip. The subtitle of this document is 'out of coercion not choice', which reflects the hesitation and confusion that had engulfed Hamas's decision-making process prior to the takeover.

12 The future of Hamas

WILL HAMAS MAINTAIN A MODERATE OR RADICAL LINE OF THINKING AND ACTION?

It all depends on the nature of the conditions, and on the political capital that Hamas's moderate leaders can acquire to present to their movement. Toning down the religious proclamations in Hamas's discourse and praxis was not an internally pain-free process, as has been shown in this book. There are certainly leaders and members within the movement who have questioned the recent line it has adopted. For example, Mahmoud Zahhar, a prominent Hamas figure and the foreign minister during the Hamas-led government, expressed to the author (in Gaza in March 2007) his dissatisfaction with the direction that his movement was taking with the national unity government. He criticized what he perceived as an 'indirect' recognition of Israel by 'some' Hamas leaders, but declined to answer what he and other dissatisfied Hamas leaders and members would do if the movement continued on its 'new path'. Until very recently, it could have been said that radical voices in Hamas were outweighed by more moderate and pragmatic ones. Those voices were prepared to restrain their discontent in the interest of the unity of the movement. The military wing, in particular, endured tremendous pressures from its 'unemployed' members. One major source of moral and political pressure was the continuous stream of accusations coming from rival groups that Hamas and its military wing had given up resistance for the sake of futile politics and governmental posts and privileges; this was exactly what the rival Fatah movement had done in previous years. Hamas's leadership was desperate to achieve concrete results from its political process, so as to sell the political route to an increasing number of its dissatisfied members.

Yet the external players, Israel, the West and Arab governments, did not help to consolidate this gradual turn within Hamas. On the contrary, a major part of their effort was directed towards bringing down Hamas's government as soon as possible, and indeed these efforts bore fruit in the West Bank, crystallizing further the political division between the West Bank and the Gaza Strip. Their short-sighted policies in imposing crippling embargos on initially the Hamas-controlled government, then the Hamas-shared unity government, may have reduced the possibility of consolidating a more politicized and pragmatic organization. The Gaza Strip/West Bank divide has further exacerbated the Palestinian weakness. With the international community only dealing with the West Bank while it continues the embargo on the Gaza Strip, positive prospects seem really minimal, if they exist at all. On the side of Hamas as a movement, both internal and external dynamics will determine whether the shift in its politics and thinking will outlive the experience of the last two years.

WILL HAMAS BE STRONGER OR WEAKER IN THE FORESEEABLE FUTURE?

It is safe to say that since its inception in late 1987 Hamas has continued on a rising curve. Certainly it has suffered setbacks and difficult times, but on the whole many successive circumstances have simply fed into the strength of the movement. By analysing those conditions propitious to the sustainable growth of the movement, an intelligent prediction can be made of whether Hamas will become stronger or weaker in the foreseeable future.

Hamas's continuing popularity and strength is intimately tied up with the continuous brutality and humiliation that the Palestinians suffer because of the Israeli occupation and Israel's refusal to acknowledge Palestinian rights. Coupled with the impact of the occupation is the failure of Hamas's rival (secular) Palestinian organizations to deliver satisfactory solutions and means of resistance against Israel. Thus, inasmuch as these two blended conditions continue to define the Palestinian reality, Hamas will sustain its power and attractiveness within the Palestinian political and popular scene.

Both being in opposition and being in power bring Hamas specific forms of good and bad fortune. When it was the leading force against the Fatah-led Palestinian Authority up to 2006, Hamas enjoyed the advantages of distancing itself from the 'dirty politics' of the Authority, and instead offered alternative ideas on how to both confront Israel without surrendering and govern the Palestinians without corruption. The more the Israeli measures continued to make the life of Palestinians hard, and the more the popularity and legitimacy of the Palestinian Authority continued to diminish, the more strength Hamas was amassing. However, being in opposition meant that Hamas was at the receiving end of continuous crackdowns by Palestinian security forces and military attacks by Israel. But if Israel and the Palestinian Authority succeeded at certain periods of time in crippling Hamas's military power, they were themselves crippled in their efforts to stem the rise of its popularity. Hamas's popularity and strength were not always joined hand in hand. A waning in its military strength would not cause a parallel drop in its popularity. On the contrary, successive (and successful) Israeli attacks did indeed weaken Hamas' military capabilities on many occasions but only served to increase its popularity.

On coming to power Hamas enjoyed some new advantages, yet ran the risk of being caught off guard with many unfamiliar challenges which could weaken its status and influence. As it assumed power in 2006 Hamas found itself for the first time in the driver's seat of the Palestinian leadership. Switching sides suddenly between opposition and authority, Hamas has become the party that is asked to deliver on major Palestinian rights and issues over which it used to accuse its Fatah rivals of selling out. As explained in this book, Hamas failed to meet the daily demands of ordinary Palestinians. Also, it acted with the logic of strict authority, taking the view that it should command respect and impose its image on people by excessive use of force if other means failed. The image of a benign and victimized movement that Hamas used to capitalize on for many years before 2006–7 was replaced by one of a harsh and determined movement that would go to extreme lengths in order to establish the form of 'order' it envisioned.

The June 2007 violent takeover of the Gaza Strip certainly shocked many Palestinians, and changed Hamas's image perhaps for ever. Although highly organized and impressively efficient, especially when compared with their Fatah rival, the Hamas military forces that managed to bring the Gaza Strip under their control in less than a week showed unexpected levels of brutality. Many cases of extrajudicial killing, torture and jailing were piled in front of many Hamas moderate leaders, who could do nothing to curb the draconian system that was immediately structured by the military wing. In terms of popularity, Hamas lost a great deal, especially in the outer circles of supporters, those who came to support Hamas out of frustration or disillusionment with Fatah. The hardcore support of Hamas, its membership and inner circles of sympathizers did not change dramatically, however. This core would remain sincere to the movement under any conditions, and regardless of whatever mistakes Hamas made. But those who stopped supporting Hamas did not automatically switch (or return) to Fatah. Fatah itself failed to present an attractive alternative during Hamas's period in power. For those who want to stop supporting Hamas, Fatah still seems as unattractive as it was on the eve of the January 2006 elections. Therefore, and in the lack of a more viable third alternative between Fatah and Hamas, the next few years are likely to bring with them more apathy, indifference and political cynicism among the Palestinians.

WHAT WILL BE THE IMPACT OF HAMAS ON MIDDLE EASTERN POLITICS AND STABILITY?

Making predictions regarding future politics in the Middle East is a typically futile exercise. Very much like shifting sands, this area is marked by a mixture of heavy external meddling and internal vulnerabilities, which produce ever-changing formations of alliances and enmities. States, parties and political players in the Middle Eastern sphere can work hard and for a long time, and end up with nothing more than ironically having served the goals of their enemies. The United States allegedly presses for democratic change in the region, and when it happens, democracy brings to power Islamist parties that can on the whole be considered as anti-American. Israel becomes anxious and troubled because Hamas wins the Palestinian elections, but exactly when Hamas finally reaches a position of political legitimacy (during its term in government from March 2006 and its power-sharing term in the national unity government until June 2007) Israeli citizens feel safer because Hamas has stopped its attacks. The fluidity and rapid pace of a seemingly endless series of major events allow for sudden rises, diversions or setbacks on the side of this party or that.

Any attempt to predict the future role and impact of Hamas in the politics of the region will suffer from these problems. However, the predictions will be most plausible if they remain firmly rooted in the reality that brought about a triumphant Hamas in the first place. This is a necessary, if not sufficient, prerequisite for any attempt at assessing the movement's future role and impact at the regional level.

Reflecting the irony and juxtapositions mentioned earlier, it was ironic that many of the propitious conditions that led to the Hamas victory in the 2006 elections were created by its enemies and rivals. Israel and the United States had greatly weakened Fatah and the Palestinian Authority, exposing them as politically incapable and damaging their credibility in the eyes of the Palestinians. In so doing, they laid the road for Hamas's march to power.

Beyond the Palestinian and Israeli context, the region as a whole has been taking on a new shape. Although it is not headed firmly in the opposite direction from the one most desired by the United States, it has partly at least been favourable to Hamas. And if the war in Iraq was meant to reshape the region toward a new US-led geopolitic, Iran has emerged as the unlikely beneficiary of influence as a result of that US intervention.

After five years of the Iraq war, Iran has come to control key aspects of internal developments in Iraq and could be a major director of its future. The Iraqi shia, who are not only the majority of the Iraqi population but also the largest group on which the United States relies in the country, would support shia Iran in any confrontation with the United States. Iran could easily play them off against the American presence there and bring the whole Iraqi quandary to a bloody new phase. In the short term at least, the United States feels almost crippled by the Iranian challenge, yet it is aware that the fate of US troops (and the whole adventure) in Iraq lies at the mercy of Iran. Because of this sudden regional leverage, Iran has gone to great lengths in publicly supporting Hamas and pledging to compensate for any cuts in the funding of Palestinian aid by the United States or the European Union.

Iran also supports Syria and Hizbullah, which in turn are strong backers of Hamas for domestic and regional reasons. Facing mounting US pressure to leave Lebanon alone, Syrians have felt cornered and compelled to undertake desperate survival measures, including public support of Hamas (as well as exploiting the Danish cartoon issue) to amass pan-Arab solidarity. The failure of the summer 2006 Israeli war against Hizbullah was considered another Iranian triumph by proxy. Along the northern Israeli–Lebanese borders there had been occasional frictions where Israeli incursions and attacks against Hizbullah bases were met by launches of rockets against Israeli cities and targets. Retaliating to the capture of two of its soldiers, and using this occasion as a pretext, Israel launched a wider war against Hizbullah in South Lebanon, aiming at eradicating the military bases of the party from that area, driving them farther north. The war failed to achieve its declared objectives, and Hizbullah emerged undefeated. Iran in the background was to be credited for this astonishing performance by Hizbullah, because of its continuous material and military support of the party over the previous years. One of the ramifications of that war was to present Hizbullah as a 'model of resistance' for other Islamist movements in the region. Hamas praised Hizbullah, and on several occasions the movement's leaders stated that they would examine how to replicate the Hizbullah model in Palestine.

Hamas in turn benefits from the rise of Iran, and not only because it could receive direct political and financial help from Tehran. It also wants to use the threat of its strong relationship with that country, however temporary its leverage might be, to entice Iran's rivals to give more help to Palestinians. Saudi Arabia, whose relationship with Hamas has always been cordial, if tacit, has become deeply worried by Iran's high-profile diplomacy, rhetoric and closeness to Hamas. Egypt is no less nervous. Along with Egypt and other Arab countries, the Saudis are struggling to prevent Hamas from falling within Iran's sphere of power, politics and ambition. Thus they are offering a diplomatic and financial hand to Hamas. Turkey too, with its moderate Islamists in power, feels that it is in an advantageous position to play a regional role, not only because its ruling elite has a shared background with Hamas but because of its friendly relations with Israel and the West.

With so many players in the region pulling strings in opposite directions, gaps are bound to be created, and Hamas should have enough skill and experience to exploit them. As long as Hamas is kept busy in Palestine and is not driven by pressures to extremes, its role and impact on regional stability will be minimal and confined to the Palestinian–Israeli conflict. Hamas has never carried out any military activity outside Palestine. However there is always the slim possibility that things could change if the movement found itself in an intractable situation. As rare and surprising as it would be for Hamas to consider military engagement beyond the Palestinian borders, Khaled Mish'al, the head of Hamas's Political Bureau, voiced a rhetorical statement that Hamas 'will fight with Iran anywhere if the latter is hit by Israel'.

If a wider military confrontation between Iran and the United States were to take place in the region, Hamas could be pushed to identify a new regional role for itself. If such a confrontation is contained, there are few reasons to think of Hamas activating itself beyond the Palestinian borders. Within them, however, whether matters will either radicalize or moderate Hamas is largely contingent on Israeli policies.

The irony of the Hamas–Israel dilemma is that when Hamas is in power, Israel enjoys more safety for its citizens. To preserve its legitimate status and focus on the pressing internal agenda, Hamas has refrained from launching attacks against Israeli targets. But Israel of course is completely distressed by Hamas's rise to Palestinian leadership. If it were to bring down Hamas's government and push it back out of power, Hamas could easily return to its military position, and another cycle of reciprocal violence could arise.

WHAT IS HAMAS'S FUTURE AFTER ITS FULL CONTROL OVER THE GAZA STRIP AND THE SEPARATION FROM THE WEST BANK?

Hamas's military seizure of power in the Gaza Strip in June 2007 and the de facto creation of a separate Hamas-controlled entity created an uncertain situation with a number of potential future scenarios. The creation of this entity meant that the Palestinians in the Occupied Territories were divided between two mini (quasi-self-ruled) but rival Palestinian entities: one in the Gaza Strip controlled by Hamas, and another in the West Bank controlled by Fatah. Needless to say, neither is fully sovereign, but both remain subjugated to the Israeli occupying power. This internal Palestinian split has elevated the factional rivalry to a deeper form of division. Although the Palestinians have suffered from the brutality of the foreign occupation for several decades, the new reality of sheer separation has taken them into a further bleak phase: facing the occupation while exceedingly disunited.

In the light of the new reality, Hamas leaders convey various and sometimes opposing views about the future of the Gaza Strip, and their role in it. Part of the leadership shows a hardline vision, insisting on opening a new chapter in the politics of the Strip, in which Hamas either stays in full control or enjoys the major part of leadership. Partisan and factional calculations are given priority in this view, because of the fear that any return to previous arrangements would be at the expense of the movement, and might risk its very existence. The 'national' justification for keeping a tight grip on power in this case draws on the argument that the Gaza Strip is more liberated from the Israeli occupation. Liberating any part of Palestine should be welcomed, and what happened in the Gaza Strip should be seen from that perspective, according to this argument. The other view within Hamas, however, is more attentive to the risks brought about by the new developments at the national level. In this view, the separation between the Gaza Strip and the West Bank is accompanied by national losses, and if it were prolonged these would counterweigh any partisan gains. Hamas leaders who take this view speak in favour of reunification even if it requires painful compromises on the part of Hamas, and express scepticism over the claims of 'liberation and achieving free control' of the Strip. Both groups would agree, alas, that any new accord with Fatah should preserve a central role for Hamas in any coming political arrangement.

From an Israeli perspective, the new division between the Gaza Strip and the West Bank serves the strategic ends of the state of Israel. It further delinks the Gaza Strip from Israel and even from the West Bank. Exporting the 'problem of Gaza' outside the realm of Israeli responsibility has for a long time been a desired strategy in itself. Also, the new geographical and political dissection deals a great blow to the Palestinian national aspiration of creating a coherent Palestinian state that includes the Gaza Strip and the West Bank as one territorial unit. In the foreseeable future the Palestinians will become consumed in their internal rivalry and affairs for long enough for Israel to solidify further realities on the ground, chief among them the Separation Wall in the West Bank, and more settlements in East Jerusalem. Even if any Gaza Strip/West Bank reunification does take place at some point in the near future, the divisions would remain deep, lurking under the surface and offering the Israelis more margins to capitalize on.

Perhaps the only risk that Israel has to deal with, as an outcome of Hamas's control over Gaza, is the further arming of Hamas, and especially its building an arsenal of small and medium-range rockets that threaten Israeli cities and towns. This risk could be addressed in various ways: continuous and unstoppable attacks on Hamas to keep the movement breathless; securing the Egyptian borders which are the main entry to Hamas and the Gaza Strip in general; and concluding an agreement, through a third party, with Hamas by which Israel keeps up the flow of certain basic supplies to the Gaza Strip, including electricity, in return for Hamas's preventing any rocket launches against Israeli cities. Yet even basic supplies from Israel will become gradually reduced in the interest of pushing the Gaza Strip towards further dependence on Egypt, in accordance with the aim of getting rid of the 'Gaza headache' entirely. In fact, many Israeli voices welcomed the reality of allowing Hamas to function as the ruling party in the Gaza Strip, combined with imposing an effective ceiling on its deliverance and military capability, and making the only exit point from the Strip to the outside world via Egypt.

An additional major risk for the Palestinians, however, that could emanate from this effective separation and southward orientation of the Gaza Strip (towards Egypt) is the potential and gradual movement of more Palestinians outside the area. The Gaza Strip is known to be the most populated place in the world, and is stricken by high levels of poverty and unemployment. A relaxed open-door policy on the Egyptian–Gazan borders, as happened when Palestinian masses brought down the border fences at Rafah, in the light of the brutal months-long blockade by Israel and the lack of ways to reunify Gaza with the West Bank, would certainly encourage massive emigration. This potential Palestinian mass movement, even if incremental, would surely appease the Israelis as it feeds into favouring their side of the demographic equation in the entire land of mandate Palestine. Because it is in their interests to encourage such migration it is not anticipated that the Israelis would allow tangible improvement in the living conditions in the Gaza Strip: various Israeli pressures are likely to continue to be imposed.

13 Hamas and the Gaza war

Was it not Hamas's insistence on (and fault in) continuing to fire rockets into the southern part of Israel that triggered the Israeli military campaign against Gaza in December 2008 and January 2009, and all that it brought upon the Palestinians, because it gave Israel an excuse to use the principle of self-defence?

Even before Hamas won the elections in January 2006, a *tahdiyeh* (truce) had been brokered by the Egyptians between Hamas and Israel. According to the truce Hamas would refrain from firing rockets in return for a reciprocal restraint by Israel, which would refrain from launching any military strikes against Gaza and Hamas. In the judgement of Israeli intelligence and military leaders Hamas showed an impressive record in keeping up with the terms of the truce and even discouraging any other Palestinian factions from undertaking rocket attacks. In return Israel exploited any chance that arose to assassinate Hamas members. The truce helped both parties, however, and it kept the violence to minimum levels. In June 2009 the truce ended and Hamas several times declared its willingness to renew it. Hamas was more than keen to keep the situation calm because it had so many other major agendas to tackle: strengthening its control over the Gaza Strip after it had seized power and defeated Fatah forces in July 2007; giving Gazans a sense of normal life; proving itself as a functioning government in Gaza, and giving top priority to dismantling the extremely harmful and inhumane blockade that has been imposed on the Gaza Strip after its election victory.

By contrast Israel had no appetite to renew the truce, and it escalated its incursions into various areas of the Gaza Strip and increased its assassination strikes on Hamas members and the movement's governmental facilities. Intensifying military pressure on Hamas was a complementary part of Israel's strategy of blockading the Gaza Strip, making the life of the people unbearable and compelling them to rise against Hamas. Hamas started to retaliate by firing rockets, carefully linking any firing to specific Israeli attacks, so that it avoided bearing the blame for the growing hostilities. Hamas felt burnt by various dilemmas, political, ideological and resistance. Politically its participation in the elections and becoming part of the Palestinian political process was not yielding concrete results to its Gazan constituencies and members; ideologically, the great transformations that it made by limiting its struggle on the West Bank and the Gaza Strip were not welcomed and rewarded internationally; and in the resistance aspect it abided by a truce which involved an effective freezing of its action and rhetoric. Refraining from reacting against the continuous Israeli military provocations would further expose Hamas. But the prevailing thinking in Israel was to keep up those provocations and refuse the renewal of the truce. Israel's plan to attack Gaza was in hand well before the date of the war in December 2008, and it needed Hamas's rockets as a convenient pretext.

Israel could have spared its southern towns Hamas's rockets if it had agreed to renew the truce on mutually acceptable terms. Some Israeli military leaders have made this point clear. Brigadier General (Retd.) Shmuel Zakai, the former commander of the Israel Defense Forces' Gaza Division, told the Israeli daily *Ha'aretz* on 22 December 2008 that:

> We could have eased the siege over the Gaza Strip, in such a way that Palestinians, Hamas, would understand

that holding their fire served their interests. But when you create a tahdiyeh [truce], and the economic pressure on the Strip continues, it's obvious that Hamas will try to reach an improved tahadiyeh, and that their way to achieve this is resumed Qassam fire.

HAS HAMAS BEEN WEAKENED BY THE WAR MILITARILY AND POLITICALLY?

Wars and armed conflicts do in many cases have unexpected consequences, often including the creation of a new reality quite different from what they were launched to achieve. This applies squarely in the case of the Israeli war against Hamas in the Gaza Strip. The outcome of the war has left Hamas stronger and with an enhanced legitimacy among the Palestinians and within the region. Israel has pursued its official goal of 'achieving a new security situation' in southern Israel with ferocity: its use of massive military force killed over 1,400 Palestinians in three weeks, most of them women and children. Yet it has failed either to silence Hamas's primitive rockets or to destroy its ability to function as a coherent entity.

In operational terms Hamas's capability has been reduced (though this may prove only temporary). Out of Hamas's strong fighters, estimated by Israeli intelligence at around 15,000, Israel killed no more than 400 in this operation. The movement's leadership remained intact, and its popular support and regional standing have risen. It is clear that in the aftermath of the war Hamas has become an unavoidable player to be included in international dialogue about the Palestinian future.

This in itself would be sufficient evidence of Israel's failure. But even as things stood, the reduction in its capacity to subdue its enemies was exposed. The army that in the six-day war in 1967 defeated the armies of four Arab states and seized parts of Egypt, Syria and Jordan which far exceeded Israel's then area has followed the embarrassment of the war against Hizbullah in 2006 with another inconclusive campaign against a non-state militia. This has an important political as well as a military dimension. The heart of Israel's strategy since Hamas's victory in the Palestinian elections of January 2006 has been the imposition of an economic blockade against Gaza, which would create such misery as to press people there to turn against the Hamas administration. What Israel ended with is world-wide condemnation and a UN report accusing it of perpetrating war crimes (Goldstone Report, September 2009).

There may be another twist of history at work here. Hamas's movement to the fore of the Palestinian national movement has been a gradual process of displacement of the previously dominant Fatah movement. Fatah's own early history after its foundation in early 1960s was also a two-track one: military (where it marched from one impasse to another: its at best patchy operations against Israel in the second half of the 1960s, its defeat by the Jordanian army in 1970, its expulsion from Lebanon in 1982) and political (where it kept moving ahead, consolidating its legitimacy and political leadership of the Palestinians).

Fatah's rise halted with the (in the end) futile peace process that started in 1991 with the Madrid conference after the war with Iraq over Kuwait. It is at the heart of what happened to Fatah that its inability to end Israel's post-1967 occupation via an endless series of negotiations came to erode its political and national capital. To put the same point in another way, the route to Palestinian legitimacy and leadership has always hinged upon offering a plausible strategy to resist and reverse the Israeli occupation. If this criterion fails to be met – as became the case for Fatah and the Ramallah-based Palestinian Authority led by the president, Mahmoud Abbas – the Palestinians will look in other directions. This suggests that long-term trends as well as short-term events are working against Fatah and for Hamas. The indications are that Palestinian opinion in the West

Bank increasingly regards Mahmoud Abbas as incapable of fulfilling the core responsibility of Palestinian leadership, and irrelevant at a time when they see their compatriots facing daily war crimes by Israel. The decline in 'Abu Mazen's' image and standing is paralleled by a growth in Hamas's popularity in the West Bank.

The pressures of war and suffering surely create exceptional circumstances, and responses that can prove fleeting. It is also certain that some Palestinians in the Gaza strip now or later will direct their anger and frustration onto Hamas, on the grounds that the movement has brought down a terrible assault upon them. But the larger and longer-term political picture is of a movement that has gained additional domestic support from the war, become regarded as a symbol of defiance and courage for millions in the Arab and Muslim worlds, and become an unavoidable reality at future diplomatic negotiations. If this is not a kind of victory, then what is?

HAS THE GAZA WAR STRENGTHENED OR WEAKENED HAMAS'S REGIONAL STANDING AND ALLIES?

The Gaza war discussed above has not only affected Hamas and the Palestinian balance of power, but also impacted regional dynamics. In his first term of office George W. Bush wanted to create a 'new Middle East'. By the end of his second term Bush had indeed created a 'new Middle East', but it was a Middle East that was almost the opposite of what he rhetorically advocated. His Middle Eastern agenda pushed down to the bottom the Palestine–Israel conflict while it prioritized crushing the Saddam Hussein regime and fighting 'terrorism'. At the same time, Israel was granted an effective carte blanche to enhance its occupation of the West Bank and the Gaza Strip which started in 1967, despite all the peace talks and proposals. All this has backfired, not only killing any idea of a peaceful 'new Middle East', but giving birth to a more 'resisting Middle East', where the moderates have been knocked out, the resistance forces have become stronger, anti-Americanism is deeper, and Palestine as the core issue in the region is as persistent as ever.

The Gaza War is, in certain ways, a result of Bush's short-sighted Middle Eastern policy: that is, to leave things to shape up in Israel/Palestine without external intervention. Things have indeed shaped up, yielding new realities where moderate Arab countries (mainly Egypt, Saudi Arabia and Jordan) are now feeling the brunt of their moderation, and gradually adopting harder stances. During the war Jordan distanced itself visibly by adopting strong language condemning Israel. During and because of this war Qatar and Turkey, both moderate allies of the United States, have become closer to the Syrian/Iranian 'axis of resistance', side by side with Hamas and Hizbullah. Although it may be only temporary, this new ad hoc regional formation materialized at the Doha summit on 16 January 2009, which was organized quickly by Qatar to orchestrate a collective Arab position against the war. While coming years will judge whether this bloc is sustainable, it is almost certain that the atmosphere in the region has shifted, because of the war, more towards a resisting Middle East. The rise of the 'new resisting Middle East' is in fact grounded in two great failures over the past two decades. The first is the Israeli failure to end its occupation of the West Bank and the Gaza Strip, especially after the historic Palestinian compromise accepting the two-state solution in 1988. The second is the American failure to adopt an even-handed policy toward Palestine/Israel, fuelling further radicalization among Palestinians, Arabs and Muslims which has helped strengthen the 'resistance' camp.

The traditional 'Arab system' hinged upon the Arab League, which although weak, fragile and fractured, has managed to sustain itself over decades. It allowed Arab countries to pretend that they were exercising politics via summit meetings and collective declarations. In so doing, this 'system' served to absorb public anger, and channel it through a new 'strategic' orientation, mostly taking its cue from Washington. On a number of occasions the 'Arab system' cracked completely, mainly over its position on the first and second American wars against Iraq, in 1991 and 2003 respectively. On the Arab–Israeli conflict it broke down after the visit of the former Egyptian President Sadat to Jerusalem in 1977 and his subsequent peace treaty with Israel. However after this the 'Arab system' used the Palestine issue as a unifying one, until the Gaza war. On this occasion, Egypt and Saudi Arabia have taken positions that have been seen by many Arabs as tacitly approving of Israel's attempt to crush, or at least weaken, Hamas. On the other side, Syria, Qatar, Iran and not unsurprisingly Turkey have taken strong positions against the Israeli war.

In dealing with large-scale crises in the region, the 'Arab system' has always offered the least effective of actions packaged with the greatest degree of rhetoric. Alas, it has maintained a sustained fragility, a status quo that allows for a minimum unified appearance although it is hollow in action. This has worked, not particularly well, but at least to the degree needed to enable it to survive. The reaction of this system to the Gaza war fell within the same maximum rhetoric/minimum action parameters. This time, however, it did not work and the system collapsed. It did indeed fracture under the scale and magnitude of the Israeli military brutality and the enormous Palestinian death toll and destruction. What makes this collapse unlike previous breakdowns of the same system is the new political environment in the region, where Iran and Turkey are eager to play a central role in regional politics. Thus the political and leadership vacuum created by Arab inaction has prompted the two 'non-Arab countries' to step in and fill the void. Both were welcomed by the vast majority of Arab public opinion, as reflected in the press, on television screens and in angry demonstrations. For some commentators, the Turkish Prime Minster

Recep Tayyip Erdogan was seen as a defiant Ottoman sultan who would never accept the humiliation of fellow Muslims, coming to the rescue with an echo of those glorious centuries. Never would either Turkey or Iran enjoy such a warm welcome by the Arab publics for any issue other than Palestine.

The Gaza summit in Doha represented the inauguration of the 'new resisting Middle East'. Seen by Egypt and Saudi Arabia as an overt attempt by Qatar to play a bigger regional role than its size merits – and one they considered intolerable – they pressured other Arab countries not to attend the summit. Angry and frustrated, the Qataris went ahead and convened the informal summit, hosting 13 Arab countries in addition to Turkey, Iran and Senegal. More daring, though, was the presence of Khaled Mish'al, Hamas's leader, Abdullah Shalla, the leader of the Islamic Jihad in Palestine, and Ahmad Jibril, the leader of a smaller leftist/pan-Arab nationalist Palestinian faction, who occupied front seats at the meeting. The strong presence of these non-state actors at a heads-of-state summit is a significant feature of the new emerging regional system.

For the Arab publics, the Doha summit proved that their governments could do much if they wanted to. The proof was that Qatar, a tiny and marginal state, was able to play a much bigger role than its size and leverage should have allowed. Nobody expected that Qatar and the 'Doha group' would declare war against Israel; but they did take a firm stance. The maximum realistic action was the freezing of Qatari and Mauritanian diplomatic relations with Israel, and threatening the withdrawal of the Arab Peace Initiative. This initiative was made by the Beirut Arab summit in 2002, and offered Israel full normalization of relations with all Arab countries, in return for accepting the two-state solution based on 1967 borders. Israel (and Bush's administration) ignored it.

Clearly, any further enhancing of the 'resistance camp' by extension or deepening is chilling news to the Egyptians and Saudis, and of course to their Western backers. The immediate

Saudi response, at a previously scheduled Arab summit in Kuwait on 19 January, convened just three days after the Doha summit, was a package of tougher language against Israel and a series of actions. It too threatened to withdraw the Arab Peace Initiative, pledged to give US$1 billion to reconstruct the Gaza Strip, reconciled with members of the 'resistance camp', Syria and Qatar, and boldly called for Palestinian unity. After the Gaza war the Arab moderate camp is on the defensive. Obama's coming to office is their last hope, that his administration might undertake a more even-handed policy which at least embraces the Arab Peace Initiative, ends the Israeli occupation and makes the creation of an independent Palestinian state a reality. If this hope fades away too, the most vivid reality in the region is the continuous rise of the 'new resisting Middle East', with Hamas as part of it, all coupled with another wave of radicalization.

Recommended reading

Abboud, Edward. *Invisible Enemy: Israel, Politics, Media, and American Culture* (Columbus, Ohio: Vox Publishing, 1997).

Abu El-Haj, Nadi. *Facts on the Ground: Archaeological Practice and Territorial Self-Fashioning in Israeli Society* (Chicago: University of Chicago Press, 2001).

Agha, Hussein and Khalidi, Ahmad S. *A Framework for a Palestinian Security Doctrine* (London: Chatham House, 2006).

Aruri, Naseer. *Palestinian Refugees: the Right of Return* (London: Pluto Press, 2001).

—— *Dishonest Broker: The U. S. role in Israel and Palestine* (Cambridge, Mass.: South End Press, 2003).

'Azza, 'Abdullah Abu. *Ma'a al-haraka al-Islamiyya fil-aqtar al-'arabiyya* [The Islamic movements in the Arab countries] (Kuwait: Al-Qalam Publishing House, 1992).

Bishara, Marwan. *Palestine/Israel: Peace or apartheid* (London, New York: Zed Books, 2001).

Christison, Kathleen. *Perceptions of Palestine: Their influence on U. S. Middle East policy* (Berkeley, Los Angeles, London: University of California Press, 1999).

Davis, Uri. *Apartheid Israel: Possibilities for the struggle within* (London and New York: Zed Books, 2003).

El-Awaisi, Abd Al-Fattah Muhammad. *The Muslim Brothers and the Palestine Question 1928–1947* (London, New York: Tauris Academic Studies, 1998).

Esposito, John L. *The Islamic Threat: Myth or reality* (Oxford: Oxford University Press, 1992).

Gee, John R. *Unequal Conflict: The Palestinians and Israel* (London: Pluto Press, 1998).

Gerges, A. Fawaz. *America and Political Islam: Clash of cultures or clash of interests* (Cambridge UK: Cambridge University Press, 1999).

Helmick, Raymond G. *Negotiating Outside the Law: Why Camp David failed* (London: Pluto Press, 2004).

Hroub, Khaled. 'A "New Hamas" through its new documents', *Journal of Palestine Studies*, vol. 35, No. 4, Summer 2006, Issue 140, pp. 6–28.

International Crisis Group. 'Islamic social welfare activism in the occupied Palestinian Territories: a legitimate target?' Middle East Report no. 13, 2 April 2003. [Online] www.crisisgroup.org/home/index.cfm?id=1662&l=1

—— 'Dealing with Hamas', Middle East Report no. 21, 26 January 2004. [Online] www.crisisgroup.org/home/index.cfm?id=2488&l=1

—— 'Enter Hamas: the challenges of political integration', Middle East Report no. 49, 18 January 2006. [Online] www.crisisgroup.org/home/index.cfm?id=3886&l=1

—— 'After Mecca: Engaging Hamas', Middle East Report No. 62, February 2007. [Online] http://www.crisisgroup.org

—— 'Inside Gaza: the challenge of clans and families', Middle East Report No. 71, December 2007. [Online] http://www.crisisgroup.org

Karmi, Ghada and Cotran, Eugene. T*he Palestinian Exodus 1948–1998* (London: Ithaca Press, 1999).

Khalidi, Rashid. *Palestinian Identity: The construction of modern national consciousness* (New York: Columbia University Press, 1997).

Khan, Mushtaq Husain (ed.) *State Formation in Palestine: Viability and governance during a social transformation* (London: RoutledgeCurzon, 2004).

Lybarger, Loren D. *Identity and Religion in Palestine: The struggle between Islamism and secularism in the Occupied Territories* (Princeton, N.J. and Oxford: Princeton University Press, 2007).

Malley, Robert and Agah, Hussein. 'Camp David: tragedy of errors', *New York Review of Books*, 9 August 2001.

Massad, Joseph. *The Persistence of the Palestine Question: Essays on Zionism and the Palestinians* (London and New York: Routledge, 2006).

Milton-Edwards, Beverly. *Islamic Politics in Palestine* (London, New York: I. B. Tauris, 1996).

Nafi, Bashir M. *Arabism, Islamism and the Palestine Question 1908–1941* (Reading, UK: Ithaca Press, 1998).

Pape, Ilan. *The Ethnic Cleansing of Palestine* (Oxford: Oneworld Publications, 2006).

Piscatori, James P. *Islam in the Political Process* (Cambridge UK: Cambridge University Press, 1983).

Powell, Jonathan. *Great Hatred, Little Room: Making peace in Northern Ireland* (London: Bodley Head, 2008).

Rogan, Eugene L. and Shlaim, Avi. *The War for Palestine: Rewriting the history of 1948* (Cambridge, UK: Cambridge University Press, 2001).

Saad-Ghorayeb, Amal. *Hizbu'llah: Politics and religion* (London: Pluto Press, 2002).

Said, Edward. S. *The Question of Palestine* (London: Vintage, 1992).

Sayigh, Yezid. *Armed Struggle and the Search for State: The Palestinian National Movement, 1949–1993* (Oxford: Oxford University Press, 1997).

Segal, Rafi and Weizman, Eyal. *A Civilian Occupation: The politics of Israeli architecture* (London: Verso, 2003).

Sha'ban, Fuad. *For Zion's Sake: The Judeo-Christian tradition in American culture* (London: Pluto Press, 2005).

Shlaim, Avi. *The Iron Wall: Israel and the Arab world* (New York, London: W. W. Norton, 2000).

Sontag, Deborah. 'Quest for Middle East peace: how and why it failed?', *New York Times*, 26 July 2001.

Tamimi, Azzam. *Hamas: A History from Within* (Massachusetts: Olive Branch Press, 2007).

Usher, Graham. *Dispatches from Palestine: The rise and fall of the Oslo peace process* (London: Pluto Press, 1999).

Yousef, Ahmad. *American Muslims: A community under siege* (Virginia: USAR Publishing Group, 2004).

Index